FRACTAL DESIGN
PAINTER 5
FOR MAC AND WINDOWS

Carol Braverman
Dawn Erdos

Henry Holt & Co., • New York

MIS:Press
A Subsidiary of Henry Holt and Company, Inc.
115 West 18th Street
New York, New York 10011
http://www.mispress.com

Limits of Liability and Disclaimer of Warranty

First Edition—1997

ISBN 1-55828-557-1

For details contact: Special Sales Director
                         MIS:Press and M&T Books
                         Subsidiaries of Henry Holt and Company, Inc.
                         115 West 18th Street
                         New York, New York 10011

10 9 8 7 6 5 4 3 2 1

Associate Publisher: *Paul Farrell*

Managing Editor: *Shari Chappell*   **Production Editor:** *Anthony Washington*
Editor: *Rebekah Young*   **Technical Editor:** *Bud Daumen*
Copy Edit Manager: *Karen Tongish*   **Copy Editor:** *Winifred Davis*

ACKNOWLEDGEMENTS

I would like to express thanks to the people who helped make my first endeavor in publishing an experience of delight and wonder.

First, I want to thank Rebekah Young, the editor, for her unswerving focus, which helped me keep the myriad bits and pieces of this project on track and moving forward smoothly. I also want to thank Danielle DeLucia for planting the seed about writing a computer book, and working with MIS:Press. Thanks also go to Cary Sullivan for her imagination in setting up the match that made this opportunity possible, and last but not least, many thanks to Paul Farrell for taking a chance on a newcomer.

On the production end, Winifred Davis has provided seamless enhancements in these pages, and Anthony Washington's abilities are reflected in the overall design of this book.

The crew at Fractal Design Corporation have lent a hand whenever needed: thanks to John Bass, Kevin Clark, and Teri Campbell. Also many thanks go to tech editor Bud Daumen for being my technical safety net.

CONTENTS-IN BRIEF

Section 1

Section 2

CONTENTS

Section 1

Section 2

SECTION 1

CHAPTER 1

GETTING
STARTED

INTRODUCTION

Welcome to Fractal Design Painter (recently renamed MetaCreations Painter). With Painter you'll be able to create artwork from scratch or alter existing images with an array of tools, materials, and effects that range from traditional methods to new digitally generated features. Together, these can be mixed and matched to create gorgeous results.

In addition to pens, pencils, chalk, pastels, oils, water colors, and the like, you now have access to other kinds of brushes such as the Image Hose and the new Photo and Gooey brushes. You can use and apply surface textures that simulate real-world papers, mimic nature, or are simply beyond classification—and you can add to this suite with your own paper texture creations! One of Painter's best features is its ability with its brushes to paint effects in situations where other programs might only allow for the click of a mouse, such as creating a mosaic painting, making a painting from a photograph by cloning, and generating truly painterly masks you can then use to apply effects or colors to your image. Painter also extends your image-editing capabilities with options that run the gamut from adjusting tonal contrast, colors, and density to such manipulations as rotating, distorting, and cropping, as well as combining different images into a composition. All of these powerful features are at your immediate disposal, and whether you are a seasoned pro or a newcomer to creating art, you'll quickly be spoiled by Painter's flexibility and ease of use.

There are many advantages to working in Painter's digital studio. You'll never run out of paint or canvas. Your brushes never require cleaning and are instantly ready for a new color. The palette consists of 16 million colors—not many traditional artists can boast of a palette like that! You don't have to be concerned about inhaling toxic chemicals. Your studio space is contained neatly on your hard drive and storage disks. You can work dry media over wet media, as when mixing colored pencils into oils, or any other unusual combination of mixed media you can think of. In addition, you can apply any painting medium to a variety of textures for different results. You can accentuate details you couldn't reach before, simply by selecting or zooming. For example, if you want to emphasize the dimples of an orange, you are not limited to real-world practicalities such as the size of your hand, the brush, or the "tooth" of the canvas.

In the digital studio, you also can try a vast array of effects on a painting without ever changing the original. Painter's tools, materials, and effects allow you to explore other options without damaging a painting. If you try something different and like a portion of the new idea but not all of it, you can selectively add that part into the original. Ultimately, Painter makes art more accessible for everyone, because the digital medium that supports it is so forgiving. You can work and rework something until you're satisfied, and it will retain its freshness.

We interviewed many artists while creating this book. Repeatedly, we heard phrases such as "it's like magic." As you'll read in Section II, many artists feel that Painter has not only changed the way they work but also the attitude and enthusiasm with which they do that work.

TECHNICAL CONSIDERATIONS

One highly praised feature of Painter is its natural, intuitive interface. First, however, we'll address a few digital topics before jumping to how to use Painter.

MACINTOSH SYSTEM REQUIREMENTS

Painter runs on all Power Mac series computers and needs Apple System 7.5 or later.

PC SYSTEM REQUIREMENTS

Painter runs on all Pentium- and 486-based computers, under Windows 95 or Windows NT 4.0.

MEMORY

Painter will run with 12 MB of application RAM, although not terribly efficiently. We recommend you use 20-plus MB and use more memory if you'll be working with multiple files or if you plan to run other programs (such as Photoshop) while you are running Painter. The Painter application takes up only about 6 MB on your hard drive, but brushes, textures, and other related files can add another 10 MB or so. Your art files can get very large—some of the art files used in this book are well over 10 MB each. It may sound a bit flippant, but use the same rule of thumb for hard disk space as for RAM—as much as you can afford.

If you plan to send large graphics files to a service bureau or printer for output, you may want to investigate a high-volume transportable system such as a cartridge drive (44 or 88 MB by SyQuest), a Bernoulli drive (44 or 90 MB by Iomega), a floptical drive (a high-capacity floppy disk using laser technology), an optical drive, or an Iomega Zip or Jaz drive. Before purchasing a transportable media drive, please check with your service bureau to make sure that it supports the system you plan to purchase.

DISPLAY

Painter is designed to run with a 24-bit color board (16 million colors), but an 8-bit board (256 colors) produces adequate results with some dithering (pixellation) of the image. If you are a perfectionist and want to see very accurate on-screen results, spring for the 24-bit board. Painter's screen redraw is comparably slow on any monitor with a less than 24-bit board.

INPUT DEVICES

You can create wonderful art using your mouse or a standard tablet, but Painter supports the use of Wacom, CalComp, Summagraphics, Hitachi, or Kurta pressure-sensitive graphics tablets. If you shop around, you can find a tablet for less than $200, and we highly recommend using one. Although you can achieve most of the effects in this book using a standard tablet or a mouse, the book assumes the use of a pressure-sensitive graphics tablet.

OUTPUT DEVICES

There is a wide variety of output options for your Painter files, from simple black-and-white laser prints to film output for process-color printing, color prints on a color laser copier or a color ink-jet printer, or an Iris printer. Because some color printers even support diverse media, your painting can be output directly onto water color paper or canvas. (Some of these output options are addressed in Chapter 13.)

LAUNCHING PAINTER FOR THE FIRST TIME

The Painter main screen is shown in Figure 1.1. If this is the first time you are launching the full version of Painter, you will be asked to personalize your software. Enter your name and the serial number (found on the inside of the program's CD jacket or on the READ ME FIRST card) and click on **OK**. If you are updating from an earlier version, you must use the new serial number found in your original package.

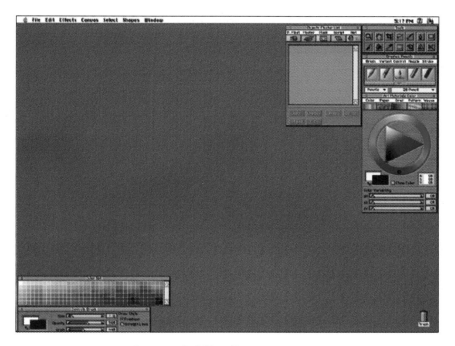

FIGURE 1.1 THE PAINTER SCREEN.

TECHNICAL SUPPORT

Some older versions of Mac INIT and DEV files can conflict with Painter. If you experience trouble installing or launching Painter, call Painter's support line at (408) 430-4200 between 8 a.m. and 5 p.m. Pacific time, Monday through Friday. You may also reach tech support via email at 2dmac@fractal.com (for Macs) and 2dwin@fractal.com (for Windows) or America Online (Keyword: Fractal). Fractal Design Corporation has a Web site at www.fractal.com.

Fractal Design Corporation is one of the few remaining software companies that offer free unlimited tech support, and their support staff is knowledgeable and, well, very supportive. We encourage you to take advantage of this fact.

STARTING A WORK SESSION

Once Painter is launched, you can create a new file or work from an existing one. Painter uses many standard menu and dialog box options for opening and saving files.

CREATING A NEW DOCUMENT

To start a new file, select **New** from the File menu. The New Picture dialog box, shown in Figure 1.2, is displayed.

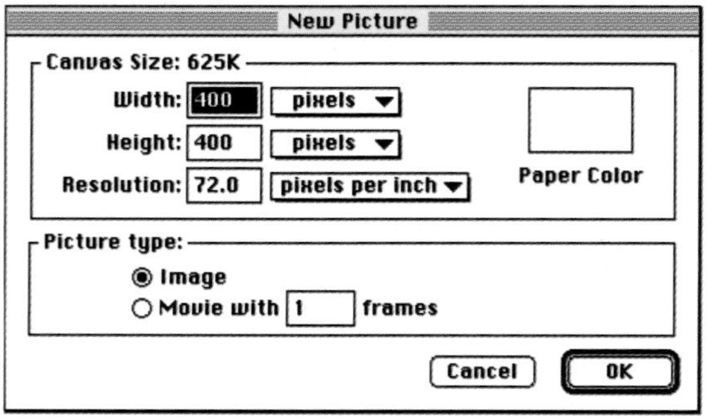

FIGURE 1.2 THE NEW PICTURE DIALOG BOX.

Enter the width and height for your image in the Width and Height fields and select the units of measurement from the pop-up menus. The default settings are for a standard 13-inch monitor.

Press the **Tab** key to move from one field to another. Click and hold on the pop-up menus to display your measurement choices; then drag to make a selection.

The Resolution setting in this dialog box specifies pixels per inch displayed on your monitor, as well as the dots per inch (dpi) rendered by your printer. Many artists work using 75 or 150 pixels per inch and then increase the resolution for output. This saves disk space and time while working—smaller files use less RAM and process faster.

The number next to Canvas Size lets you know how much memory your file is using. Reducing the width, height, or resolution results in a smaller image size; increasing them results in a larger image size.

Click on the square above Paper Color to select the paper background color for your image. The standard color selector for the Mac is shown in Figure 1.3.

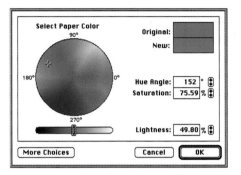

FIGURE 1.3 THE STANDARD COLOR SELECTOR.

Select your background color by entering values or clicking on the color wheel. Click on **OK**. The background color is now displayed in the Paper Color window. If you are creating a still image, click on the **Image** radio button. If you are creating a movie or animation, select the **Movie with __ frames** radio button and enter the number of frames in the corresponding field. (Please see Chapter 11 for more information on movies and animation.)

Click on **OK** and a new window is opened. Your canvas is ready, and you're all set to paint.

OPENING AN EXISTING DOCUMENT

You may open files saved in the following formats: RIFF, TIFF, PICT, Photoshop 4.0, Photoshop 3.0, BMP, PCX, Targa, GIF, JPEG, or Pyramid. You can't open an EPS file (see Chapter 13 for more information on file formats and Painter). This makes it easy to work with files that have been created or modified in other programs (such as Dabbler, Poser, Photoshop, or Detailer). Please note, however, that files must be saved in RGB color format to be opened in Painter.

To open an existing file, select **Open** from the File menu. The dialog box shown in Figure 1.4 is displayed. Locate the file you want to open. If the file was saved using Painter, Detailer, or Dabbler, you'll see a thumbnail preview in the right side of this dialog box.

Below the preview window, you'll see file information for every document (even those not created in Painter): the file dimension in pixels, how much memory is used, and the file type.

Click on **Browse** to display thumbnails of all Painter files in the folder you currently have selected, as shown in Figure 1.5.

Windows users must select a file before clicking the Browse button.

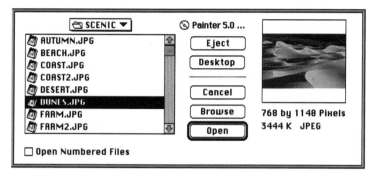

FIGURE 1.4 THE FILE OPEN DIALOG BOX.

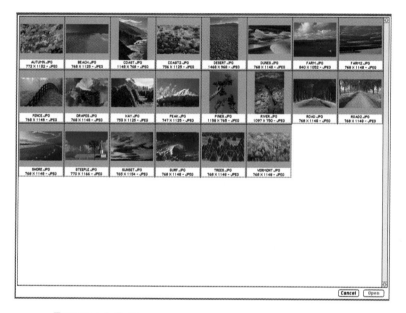

FIGURE 1.5 BROWSING THE CONTENTS OF A FOLDER.

The Open Numbered Files option automatically creates a Painter frame stack from sequentially numbered files to generate a Painter movie. (Please see Chapter 11 for more information on this feature.)

To open a file from the main File Open dialog box or from the Browse dialog box, select the file and click **Open** or double-click on your selection.

SAVING A DOCUMENT

To save your work, select **Save As** from the File menu. The Save As dialog box, shown in Figure 1.6, is displayed.

FIGURE 1.6 THE SAVE AS DIALOG BOX.

Select the location for your art files and enter a file name in the Save Image As (Mac) or File Name (Windows) field.

Select the file format from the Type (Mac) or Save As Type (Windows) pop-up menu. Figure 1.7 shows your file type choices. Descriptions of each file type Painter supports are listed in Chapter 13.

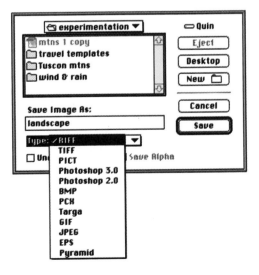

FIGURE 1.7 FILE TYPE OPTIONS.

The RIFF type is Painter's native file format. To keep your creative options open, its a good idea to save your document in RIFF, especially in its early stages, because the RIFF format supports certain Painter features such as plug-in floaters and mosaics. When you're sure your image is set, then save it in another file format.

MOVING AROUND PALETTES AND DRAWERS

Translating real-world media and related information into the digital realm is done through Painter's palettes and dialog boxes. Thereare so many tools, materials, effects, and options to work with, that it can get confusing. Subpalettes, drawers, secondary palettes, dialog boxes, and extra windows are nested in several of the essential palettes listed on the main screen under Window. All this information can be overwhelming even to the most experienced user. So, for clarity's sake, let's pause for a moment and to differentiate between the features.

First, there are the six main palettes: Tools, Brushes, Art Materials, Objects, Controls, and Color Set. The Brushes, Art Materials, and Objects palettes branch out to subpalettes, represented by icons at the top of the palette window. You can select a subpalette by clicking on its icon.

Subpalettes have drawers or interactive features such as sliders, radio buttons, pop-up menus, or lists; what you'll be using each of them for will be covered in later chapters. Secondary palettes are reached through the Brushes: Control subpalette menu. These are a specialized group of palettes used for fine-tuning brushes (see Chapter 5).

Drawers are a big part of Painter's interface, and recognizing whether a drawer is open or closed will save you some time and effort at the beginning. You can tell you're in a drawer when you see a blue horizontal bar underneath the icons. When the bar is a solid blue, and the triangle in its center is pointing downward, you are in the closed portion of the drawer. When the triangle in the center of the bar is green, and pointing upward, you are in the expanded portion of the drawer. Figure 1.8 shows the drawer closed and expanded.

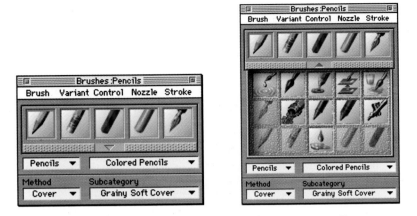

FIGURE 1.8 THE CLOSED AND EXPANDED DRAWERS OF THE BRUSHES PALETTE.

When you have made your choices in the expanded drawer, you can close it. The major advantage of this is additional real estate on your desktop. You can streamline the drawer's size even more by clicking on the zoom box in the upper-right corner of the window.

Painter's palettes, subpalettes, drawers, secondary palettes, and dialog boxes are very interactive, as you'll soon discover. This interactivity means that you can be in one window and make choices in others, allowing you to experiment with a variety of features while in preview mode. For example, if you choose Effects: Color Overlay, you can click on the Color palette and choose another color. Then you can move onto the Paper palette to choose another paper texture.

CUSTOMIZING YOUR WORKSPACE

Painter has wonderful features that help you feel comfortable in the digital environment. You can set up preferences to suit your way of working and organize your workspace for ease of use.

ESSENTIAL PALETTES

Paring down the number of palette windows you'll need to get started is a good way to become comfortable within the Painter environment. The windows you will need on your desktop at all times are the Art Materials palette, the Brushes palette, the Tools palette, and the Controls palette. If they appear on your desktop, close the Objects and Color Set palettes for now. Figure 1.9 shows these palettes arranged around the working document.

FIGURE 1.9 ARRANGING PALETTES.

If your monitor is smaller, you can tuck palettes behind each other and access them quickly, by clicking on them.

SETTING PREFERENCES

Modifying several items right away will help you settle into your working environment. You can change the direction of the brush pointer and, on the Macintosh, change its color as well. To do this, go to Edit: Preferences: General, and change the settings in the dialog box that appears.

Painter allows you up to 32 levels of Undo, affording you immense flexibility when you're immersed in your work. The default setting is 5, and be forewarned that the higher the setting, the more memory is eaten up. To change this setting, bring up the Undo dialog box, which is found under Edit: Preferences: Undo.

If you work with a stylus, you will want to get into the habit of using the Brush Tracking dialog box at the beginning of each work session. Go to Edit: Preferences: Brush Tracking, and scribble or stroke on your tablet. Figure 1.10 shows the Brush Tracking dialog box in action.

Painter reads the pressure and speed of your stroke, then adjusts this sensitivity across the board to all the pressure-sensitive brushes you will use during this work session. Remember that the default setting is restored every time you quit out of the program.

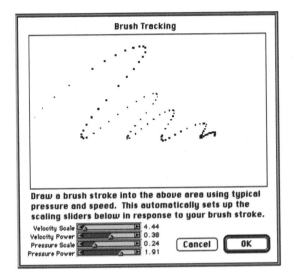

FIGURE 1.10 THE BRUSH TRACKING DIALOG BOX.

There's another feature that will help you feel a little more comfortable within this digital environment: you can rotate your document in its window the same way you might do if you were drawing or painting with real-world materials. Refer to Chapter 2 for a detailed explanation of the Rotate Page tool.

TEAR-OFF PALETTES

By popular demand, Painter has reinstated tear-off palettes. With more than one subpalette open at the same time, you can view your latest choices and make changes without having to switch back and forth. (This saves some time and aggravation.) To tear off a subpalette, simply drag it to another place on your screen. Painter won't allow you to tear off the currently selected subpalette, so you'll first have to select another icon, and then tear off the one you want.

CUSTOM PALETTES

You can create your own palettes that suit your style and/or hold items for a particular assignment. Any art material, brush, script, plug-in floater, or menu command can be placed on a new palette. Painter makes aliases of each item, so use any item as often as you wish—you can't harm the defaults unless you deliberately delete them.

To create a custom palette, choose **Window: Custom Palette: Add Command**, and in the Add to field, choose **New**. Figure 1.11 shows the

Custom palette dialog box. You can also drag an icon off its palette to automatically create a custom palette.

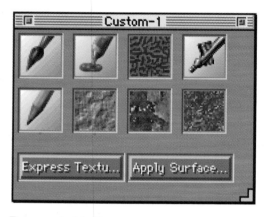

FIGURE 1.11 CREATING A CUSTOM PALETTE.

It is also through this dialog box that menu items are added to your custom palette. Open the dialog box, move anywhere around the program to select your choice, and a button containing the item will appear on your custom palette.

Creating custom palettes is an enticing possibility, and the Custom Palette Organizer helps you manage them in a clear-cut way. Figure 1.12 shows the Custom Palette Organizer, which you access under Window: Custom Palette: Organizer.

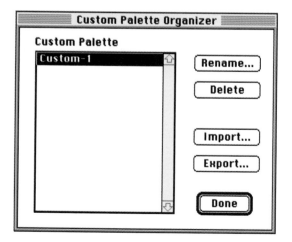

FIGURE 1.12 THE CUSTOM PALETTE ORGANIZER.

Select the custom palette to rename it, export it to another folder, or delete it, by following the prompts in the dialog box. The Import button loads the custom palettes you've saved into another folder.

To maximize the available work space, Painter enables a vertical or horizontal design of the custom palette through keyboard commands and dragging. To move an item, hold down the **Control-Shift** (Mac) or **Command-Shift** (Windows) keys, and simply drag each item into position. To delete an item, hold down the **Control-Shift-Option** (Mac) or **Command-Shift-Alt** (Windows) keys, and when the cursor changes into a tiny trash can, click on the item you want to remove.

PALETTE LAYOUTS

Painter has another way to make this dense environment feel a little more like home. With all these palettes to work with, sometimes you'll be shuffling them around, opening and closing a number of them as your work progresses. When you close out of Painter and open it again, you'll see the palettes arranged as you left them.

Good news. You can set up your ideal palette arrangement by selecting **Window**: **Arrange Palettes: Save Layout**. You will be prompted to name the layout, and it will be stored on the Arrange Palettes list, ready to be selected any time you need it. The next time there's some tidying up to do, let Painter reshuffle for you while you get ready to work.

LIBRARIES AND MOVERS

Painter organizes brushes, paper textures, patterns, gradations, weaves, color sets, brush looks, nozzles, floaters, selections, lighting, and scripts into libraries. When you first open Painter, you're initially working with the default libraries. The program ships with additional libraries you can load. The Load Library command is located at the bottom of the each palette's cascading menu.

You can also create libraries, and as you become more familiar with the tools, materials, and effects, you'll probably need to create some libraries, because you'll be adding variants that reflect your personal style.

Movers are the dialog boxes that enable you to create and manage libraries. All movers function the same way. In Chapter 5, you will find a complete run-through of how to use the Brush Mover so that you'll be able to use Movers whenever you need them.

CHAPTER 2

THE TOOL PALETTE

FIGURE 2.1 THE TOOLS PALETTE.

INTRODUCTION TO THE TOOLS PALETTE

Painter is simple and straightforward to use, yet it also has many complex and sophisticated features. The Tools palette is a perfect example: its arrangement is remarkably clear-cut and compact. On the right side are all the tools that relate to selecting, and the various tools that will help you perform basic functions and access additional capabilities are on the left (Figure 2.2).

FIGURE 2.2 THE TOOLS PALETTE'S ARRANGEMENT.

As you'll see in Figure 2.3, tools with similar functions are nested together in the Tools palette. When you see a tiny black triangle in the lower right corner, you can find additional tool choices by holding down the stylus or mouse and dragging to the icon.

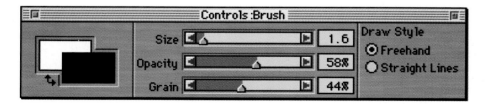

FIGURE 2.3 THE FULL ARRAY OF TOOLS.

Before we go further, let's make sure the Tools palette is visible on your screen; it should be displayed in the upper-right corner when you launch the program. If it's not, select **Tools** from the Windows menu.

THE CONTROLS PALETTE

Working hand-in-hand with the Tools palette is the Controls palette, shown in Figure 2.4.

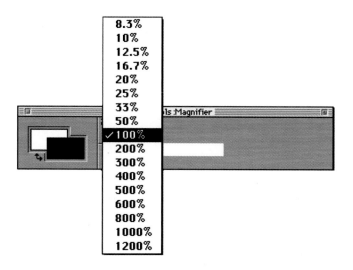

FIGURE 2.4 THE CONTROLS PALETTE.

To choose a tool, click on its icon once. Each time you select a tool, the Controls palette changes to reflect the currently selected tool. Sometimes the Controls palette offers information (such as the RGB values for a selected color), and other times it displays pop-up menus, sliders, or radio buttons so you can fine-tune the chosen tool some more. You'll get a better feel for this as we go through each tool on the Tools palette.

Let's start with the six items on the left side of the palette: the Magnifier, Grabber, Crop, Dropper, Paint Bucket, and Brush tools.

Magnifier Tool

The Magnifier tool lets you zoom in and out of an image, changing your view as you need to see details or the picture as a whole. Click on the Magnifier tool to select it. Place the cursor over the area you want to view. Notice that it changes to a magnifying glass with a plus sign (+) in the middle when you move it over

your active window. Click once, and Painter magnifies the area. The magnification factors progress in the same increments as shown under the Zoom Level option on the Controls palette, from 8.3% to 1200% (see Figure 2.5).

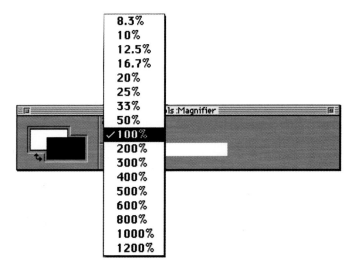

FIGURE 2.5 PAINTER'S ZOOM FACTORS.

The magnification factor is indicated in the title bar of your window; for example, it may read **Untitled @ 200%**.

To zoom out, place the Magnifier cursor in the active window, and hold down the **Option** key (Mac) or the **Alt** key (Windows), and click in the area you want to reduce. Notice that the plus sign in the magnifying glass cursor changes to a minus sign (–).

Your image zooms out in the same increments that it zoomed in. You can also click and drag with the Magnifier tool to zoom into a particular area.

As in other programs, you can temporarily switch to the Magnifier tool through a keyboard command while another tool is selected (except for the Text tool). To zoom in, hold down **Command-Spacebar** (Mac) or **Ctrl-Spacebar** (Windows) and click in the area you want to view. To zoom out, hold down **Command-Option-Spacebar** (Mac) or **Ctrl-Alt-Spacebar** (Windows). Double-clicking on the Magnifier tool icon restores the image to 100%.

Grabber Tool and Rotate Page Tool

The Grabber tool and the Rotate Page tool share the same space in the toolbox. The Grabber tool moves your image around in its window, regardless of whether you have enlarged it through zooming.

To use the Grabber tool, select it, and then click and drag the hand icon in your document window, releasing the mouse or stylus when the image is positioned where you want it.

You can temporarily change to the Grabber tool while another tool (except for the Text tool) is selected by holding down the **Spacebar**.

The Rotate Page tool was developed to accommodate artists who are used to turning a page as they work. With this tool selected, click on the page you want to rotate. You'll see a large box with an arrow in it. Drag your cursor to rotate the arrow in the direction you want your page to turn, and then release the cursor button. To return to the regular upright view, simply click once on the image while the Rotate Page tool is selected. Figure 2.6 shows the Rotate Page tool in action.

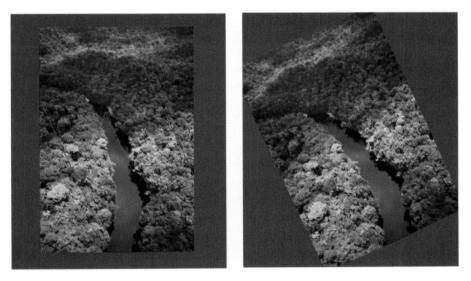

FIGURE 2.6 USING THE ROTATE PAGE TOOL.

Crop Tool

With the Crop tool you can edit your image by eliminating unwanted portions. To use the Crop tool, select it and then drag in the image over the area you want to save. You will see a selection marquee. To modify the cropping area horizontally or vertically, drag your mouse or stylus on a horizontal or vertical line of the marquee. Notice that when you do this, the crosshair icon will change to a two-way arrow.

If you want to change the dimension of the cropping box in two directions at once, place the cursor over a corner and drag in the direction you want to add or subtract to the cropping box. This time, the crosshair icon will change to a diagonal two-way arrow.

Checking the Aspect Ratio option in the Controls palette and entering values in the field boxes enables you to create perfectly proportioned rectangles. If you want to restrict the proportion of the cropping box to a perfect square, hold down the **Shift** key when you drag.

When the cropping box is correctly positioned over the portion of the image you want to keep, move the cropping icon inside the box, where it will change to active, cutting scissors. Click once with the stylus or mouse, and everything outside the box is deleted.

Dropper Tool

The Dropper tool lets you select a color from one area of the image to use on another area, or to get a color from another open file. When you use the Dropper tool, the chosen color becomes the current color on the Art Materials: Color palette.

There are two rectangles on the lower left of the palette—make sure the front one, the Foreground indicator, is selected, as in Figure 2.7.

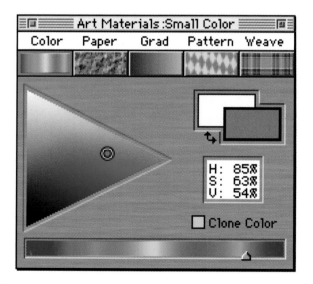

FIGURE 2.7 ACTIVATING THE CURRENT COLOR ON THE ART MATERIALS: COLOR
PALETTE. THE OVERLAPPING COLORS ARE ALSO VISIBLE ON THE CONTROLS PALETTE.

You can temporarily switch to the Dropper tool when working with the Brush tool, Paint Bucket tool, Floating Adjuster tool, or Crop tool, by pressing the **Command** (Mac) or **Ctrl** (Windows) key.

Now all you have to do is select a brush, and you're ready to paint with the selected color.

Paint Bucket Tool

The Paint Bucket tool acts as a fill tool, allowing you to apply color to the entire image, a selection, or a specific area. You can use the Tolerance and Feather sliders on the Controls palette to control the range of the fill and the softness of its edges.

When you drag with the Paint Bucket tool, you create a rectangle that is automatically filled with the current color. Double-clicking on the Paint Bucket tool icon brings up a dialog box that allows you to further control your fill by locking unwanted color out of the area. (Chapter 3 covers this tool in more detail.)

Brush Tool

Here's where Painter's magic begins. Select the Brush tool to access all of your painting and drawing tools. Please note that, unlike other painting programs, choosing this tool in the toolbox simply places you in the painting mode: it is in the Brushes palette that you will find limitless choices for painting and drawing. You also change to the brush icon automatically when you choose a new brush in the Brushes palette. Chapters 4 and 5 cover brushes in detail.

Now let's look at the eight tools nested on the right side of the toolbox. Don't forget to keep looking at the Controls palette as we cover each tool to see the additional choices Painter provides.

Lasso Tool

The Lasso tool is used for making freehand selections. Just click and drag the area you want to select. If the end point and the original point of your lasso selection are not connected, Painter will automatically join the points and complete the selection for you.

You can add to a selection by holding down the **Shift** key as you redraw with your stylus or mouse. To subtract from a selection, hold down the **Command** (Mac) or **Ctrl** (Windows) key.

Magic Wand Tool

The Magic Wand tool generates color-based masks and selections for you quickly. To use the Magic Wand tool, simply click in your image with the stylus or mouse.

You can increase and decrease the color range of the Magic Wand by adjusting the Tolerance and Color Feather sliders in the Control palette. You can add to a selection by holding down the **Shift** key as you draw with your stylus or mouse.

Pen and Quick Curve Tools

The Pen tool and the Quick Curve tool are used to draw shapes, and they share the same space in the toolbox. The Pen tool uses a combination of straight lines and Bezier curves to create a path with points that can then be edited. The Quick Curve tool creates freehand paths, and does not include straight lines.

To close paths made by the Pen and the Quick Curve tools, connect the end point with the original point, or click on the **Close** button in the Controls palette. To change the path you've just created into a selection, click on the **Make Selection** button in the Controls palette.

Rectangular and Oval Shape Tools

The Rectangular Shape tool and the Oval Shape tool share the same space in the toolbox. These tools function identically, allowing you to create rectangular and elliptical shaped paths, which can be edited or made into floaters and selections.

To restrict the proportions to a square or circle, hold down the **Shift** key when drawing with the Rectangular Shape tool or the Oval Shape tool.

Shape Edit Tools

The Scissors tool, Convert Point tool, Add Point tool, and Remove Point tool share the same to space in the toolbox. Together, they enable you to edit paths in specific ways so that you can fine-tune them.

The Scissors tool lets you cut out a portion of a shape path whether it is open or closed. Once you cut a closed path, it becomes open. The Convert Point tool lets you change a curved point to an uncurved point, and vice versa. The Add Point tool lets you click on the path to create a new point, and the Remove Point tool lets you delete a point by clicking on an existing point.

Floating Adjuster, Selection Adjuster, and Shape Selection Tools

The Floating Adjuster, Selection Adjuster, and Shape Selection tools share the same space in the toolbox. Their functions are quite distinct. Refer to Chapter 6 for greater detail on all three of these tools.

The Floating Adjuster works with floaters and shapes, and operates hand-in-hand with the Controls palette's opacity slider and compositing method options.

The Selection Adjuster tool enables you to transform selections. You can change a selection's size and proportions or rotate a selection. Additionally, you can feather a selection via the Mask menu on the Objects palette.

The Shape Selection tool is very useful: it allows you to modify the points of a path. You can move points on a path or shift the length and direction of a point's handles to change the overall shape. You also use the Shape Selection tool to group floaters.

Text Tool

The Text tool adds text to your images, as in Figure 2.8.

FIGURE 2.8 ADDING TEXT.

In the Controls palette you can choose a font, size it (point size), and space the letters apart (tracking). Chapter 6 covers text in greater detail.

Selection Tools

The Rectangular Selection and Oval Selection tools share the same space in the toolbox.

Double-click on the Rectangular Selection tool to select the entire image or choose **All** from the Select menu. Click and drag to select a particular area in your image. To deselect an area, choose **None** from the Select menu, or double-click on the Selection tool icon in the toolbox.

As you would elsewhere, to restrict the proportions to a perfect square or a circle, hold down the **Shift** key.

Also, if you're not happy with the selection you've made, you can adjust the boundaries of a selected area by adding or subtracting from it. To add to your selection, hold down the **Shift** key and drag, as shown in Figure 2.9. To subtract, hold down the **Command** (Mac) or **Ctrl** (Windows) key.

FIGURE 2.9 ADJUSTING THE BOUNDARIES OF A SELECTED AREA.

CHAPTER 3

COLOR

This chapter covers the basics for selecting and using color in Painter, including the digital broad sweeps of color that you can produce without picking up a brush. All colors that we see are our perception of different wavelengths of light. Almost all colors can be created by using one of three color-mixing systems, each of which is best suited for a different purpose.

❏ **RGB**. In the RGB color system, color is created by the light source of your color monitor or color TV. Red, green, and blue phosphors overlap and vary in intensity and brightness to form clusters that we commonly refer to as *pixels*. In Painter, you have the option of working in this color mode by selecting **RGB Colors** from the Color palette's Color Picker list, which you'll find under the Color menu.

❏ **HSV**. The HSV color system is based upon the way the human eye perceives color. *Hue* is the color itself, *saturation* refers to the degree of the color's intensity, and *value* is associated with the color's relative degree of brightness. Painter uses the HSV system as the referential standard to talk about color.

❏ **CMYK**. The CMYK color system refers to reflective color, color that is created by printing ink onto paper. Cyan, magenta, yellow, and black are separated to four plates that are then combined to produce a standardized range of color when printed. Painter does not support the CMYK color mode to work in, but through a color management system, described later in this chapter, Painter helps you prepare your documents if you intend to print them later on.

Remember, Painter mixes paint on the Color palette using HSV and saves files in RGB format. It does not use CMYK. If you need to use the CMYK color system because you plan to import your files into a page layout program or output to RC paper or film for four-color process printing, you must save your Painter files as EPS DCS files, which are CMYK. This format is discussed in Chapter 13.

THE COLOR PALETTE

The Color icon on the Art Materials palette is your primary means of selecting and creating colors. Click on the icon and the zoom box in the upper-right corner of the palette window to display the expanded color palette, shown in Figure 3.1.

If your palette doesn't look like the one in Figure 3.1, select **Standard Colors** from the Color: Color Picker menu on the Art Materials palette.

FIGURE 3.1 THE EXPANDED COLOR PALETTE.

SELECTING COLORS

You create colors using both the spectrum ring and the triangular color picker. The spectrum ring selects the dominant hue, and the triangle represents the range of saturation and value (brightness) for that hue. Drag the selection circle on the triangle to select saturation and brightness. Moving the circle to the right increases the color's intensity, and moving the circle to the left decreases the color, so the extreme tip of the triangle will give the most saturated color and the extreme left will desaturate it to gray. Moving the circle up will brighten the color, and moving it down will darken it.

Together, the spectrum ring and triangular color picker represent 16 million colors to choose from.

PRIMARY AND SECONDARY COLORS

The two rectangles on the Color palette represent the primary and secondary colors. In Painter terms, the words *primary* and *secondary* refer to first and second choices, unlike other programs in which similar icons represent foreground and background colors. (The background color in Painter is the paper color you choose when creating a new document, and its default is white when working with existing images.)

Most of the time you'll be working with the primary, or current, color. However, depending on the brush you choose, your strokes can contain both the primary and secondary colors, and the range of colors in between them.

Click on the front rectangle on the lower-left portion of the Color palette to select your primary painting color, and then on the back rectangle to select your secondary painting color. Click again on the front rectangle. Figure 3.2 shows blue as the primary color (front rectangle) and yellow as the secondary color (back rectangle).

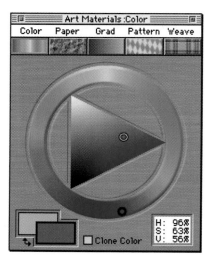

FIGURE 3.2 THE COLOR PALETTE WITH BLUE SELECTED AS THE PRIMARY COLOR AND YELLOW SELECTED AS THE SECONDARY COLOR.

To increase the color range of a brush stroke, open the Sliders palette, which you'll find under the Control menu on the Brushes palette. When the Color slider is set to **None**, you can only paint with one color, but by changing settings you can use both the primary and secondary colors for varied results. You can also use primary and secondary colors when working with two-point gradations.

PAINTING WITH MULTIPLE COLORS

You can also set up your Color palette to paint using more than two colors by using the HSV Color Variability sliders on the bottom of the expanded Color palette.

❑ Increase the ± H (hue) percentage to add more hues to your brush stroke.

❏ Increase the ± S (saturation) percentage to add more variations of saturation to a brush stroke.

❏ Increase the ± V (value) percentage to add more variations of lights and darks in a brush stroke.

Your kaleidoscopic selection is previewed in the front rectangle, as shown in Figure 3.3. Figure 3.4 shows some multicolored brush strokes.

FIGURE 3.3 SELECTING A MULTICOLORED BRUSH STROKE.

FIGURE 3.4 MULTICOLORED BRUSH STROKES.

COLOR SETS

Painter recognizes that artists traditionally begin their work with a set color palette. For this reason, Painter provides a Color Set window for choosing colors and a Color Set palette for loading default color sets, creating new ones, and other management options.

To open the Color Set window of color squares, go to Windows, on the Main menu bar, and select **Show Color Set**. To open the Color Set palette, go to the Art Materials: Color palette, and under the Color menu, select **Adjust Color Set**. Figure 3.5 shows the Color Set window and the Color Set palette.

To open an existing color set, click the **Library** button, select the set you want to open (from the Colors, Weaves, and Grads folder for the Mac or the Colors folder for Windows), and click **OK**. Figure 3.6 shows the Pantone Color Set window and the Color Set palette.

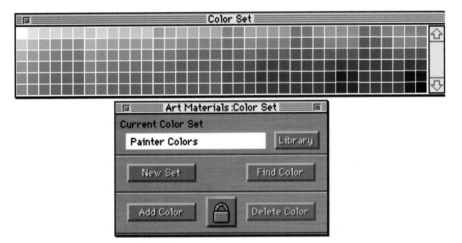

FIGURE 3.5 THE COLOR SET WINDOW AND THE COLOR SET PALETTE.

You can create a new color set based on the colors in an existing image. Click the **New Set** button to create an empty set. With the image open and using the Dropper tool, select a color to add to the set. Click the **Add Color** button, and keep alternating between choosing a color and clicking the Add Color button to expand your new color set. To delete a color, select it with the Dropper tool, and then click on the **Delete Color** button. If you would like to name the colors in a set, double-click on the color, enter a name, and click **OK**. When you are through, click on **New Set** to name and save the new set, following the prompts to name and store the set.

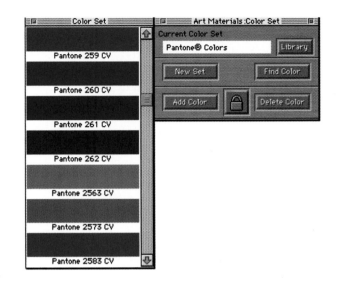

FIGURE 3.6 THE PANTONE COLOR SET AND THE COLOR SET PALETTE.

These controls may also be used to edit existing color sets. The **Find Color** button lets you search a set (by name) for a particular color. The options on the expanded palette, shown in Figure 3.7, allow you to customize the way your sets are displayed.

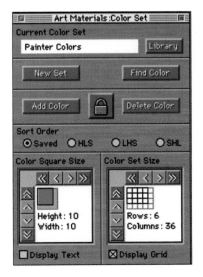

FIGURE 3.7 THE EXPANDED COLOR SET PALETTE.

The Color Square Size options allow you to change the width and height of the squares in the Color Set window. Check **Display Text** to have color names displayed below each color square.

The Color Set Size options let you change the window's arrangement horizontally and vertically. Check **Display Grid** to place a thin line between color squares.

ANNOTATING COLORS

The Annotation feature labels colors in your image (even on floaters) based on the names in a color set. Annotations "float" over your image and can be saved in files using Painter's native RIFF format.

Be sure the Show Annotations option on the Canvas menu is toggled on. Select **Annotate...** from the Annotations cascading menu on the Canvas menu. Click on the color you want to annotate. A dialog box with a Done button is displayed. Ignore it for now and drag your cursor off the color. Release the cursor, and the annotated name is displayed. Continue annotating colors in this manner.

To delete an annotation, select its label and press **Delete** (Mac) or the **Backspace** key (Windows).

When you have completed your annotations, click the **Done** button. Figure 3.8 shows an image being annotated.

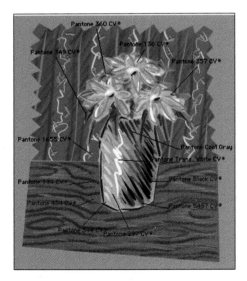

FIGURE 3.8 ANNOTATING THE COLORS IN AN IMAGE.

POSTERIZING WITH COLOR SETS

Some work, such as multimedia, Web graphics, or textile design calls for a reduced color palette. You can posterize an image or a floater (see Chapter 6 for information on floaters) by first creating your set of colors. Next, under Effects, on the Main menu bar, scroll down to Tonal Control, and choose **Posterize Color Set**. Painter automatically updates your image or selected floater by translating the original colors to their closest counterparts in the new color set based upon their hue, saturation, and value.

CLONING COLORS

You can *clone*, or copy, a color or an area of colors from existing imagery to another place, either in a new document or within the same painting. First, click on the Color palette's **Clone Color** option or select a Cloner brush (see Chapter 8 for more information on cloning brushes) to automatically activate the Clone Color option. Next, select the color or color area you want to copy by clicking in the image while holding down the **Control** (Mac) or **Shift** (Windows) key, and then paint elsewhere with your stylus or mouse. Your source image is re-created via the variant you selected, as Figure 3.9 shows.

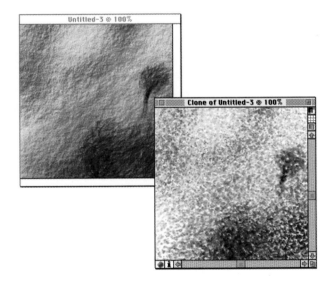

FIGURE 3.9 A SOURCE IMAGE (LEFT) AND ITS CLONED COLORS (RIGHT) USING THE IMPRESSIONIST CLONER VARIANT.

37

THINKING AHEAD TO OUTPUT

The digital environment, with its colorful palette of 16 million colors, offers us so much latitude for creativity that we sometimes lose track of real-world restrictions.

COLORS FOR PRINT

Although you have a palette of 16 million colors to paint with, an offset printing press cannot print every color you see on your screen. To stay within the confines of printable reality as you work, you'll need to view your RGB image in CMYK mode at some point. Otherwise, when it's time to output your work, you might be in for a potentially expensive and time-consuming surprise after all your effort. As yet, there is no universal, standard system for gauging color output; that is, because of the different types of scanners, monitors, and printers, it is difficult to predict the final output. Therefore, Painter, together with Kodak, have set up a system that will anticipate an optimal preview of how your image will print in CMYK, by having you select from lists of input, display, and output devices that match or are close substitutes of what you are using.

The implementation of the system is flexible: you can begin a project with this system set up, check in from time to time as your work progresses, or convert it when you are through. To set up the controls, go under Canvas on the Main menu bar, select **Output Preview** from the cascading menu, and scroll down to select **Kodak Color Correction**. This opens the Select Profiles dialog box, which gives you three pop-up menus for each phase of production. If your type is not represented on the list, choose an acceptable alternative such as **Generic**, or choose **None**. When you're through, click **OK** and your image, the Color palette, and the color icons will be updated. Figure 3.10 shows the Select Profiles dialog box.

FIGURE 3.10 THE SELECT PROFILES DIALOG BOX.

The third icon on the upper-right corner of your document window allows you to switch back and forth between preview mode and nonpreview mode as you work. If you want to deselect the **Output Preview** altogether, go to Preview Options, at the bottom of the Canvas menu list, to open the **Select Profile** dialog box. Set the options to **None** in the pop-up menus.

Another option to help you gauge color printability is Show Gamut Warning, also found in the Select Profile dialog box. When you check the option and click OK, your image is overlaid with the gamut color to indicate areas that will print poorly, so that you can go ahead and make the necessary tonal adjustments. Remember, Painter saves documents in RGB: you are simply previewing through a refined system that gives an optimal idea of how your art will print. To save your document as CMYK, you have to save it in the EPS format.

Painter does not open documents saved as EPS, so it is advisable to also save a version in a different format for future work. For information on printing with the Kodak Color Management System, refer to Chapter 13.

WARNING

COLORS FOR VIDEO

As with offset printing presses, not all colors displayed on your monitor can be used in video. However, most colors on your monitor will be video-legal (except bright yellows and cyan blues).

Open the Effects menu and select **Video Legal Colors...** from the Tonal Control cascading menu. You'll see a preview of the video-legal image in the dialog box shown in Figure 3.11. Select either the **NTSC** (United States) or **PAL** (European) video system from the pop-up menu and click **OK**.

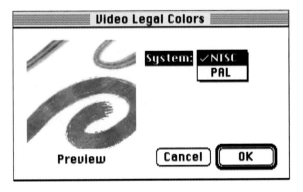

FIGURE 3.11 THE VIDEO LEGAL DIALOG BOX.

You may also apply video-legal colors to a selected area of an image by selecting the area before selecting Video Legal Colors.

SWEEPS OF COLOR

Now that you're working in the digital environment, you can quickly generate large areas of color, covering either an entire image, a selected part of it (see Chapter 6 for more detail on selections), or a cartoon cel. You can fill your choice with a single color, a clone source if one is chosen, a gradation, a pattern, or a weave, by using either the Paint Bucket tool or the Fill command. (You can also fill with special effects, which we'll get into in Chapter 7.)

THE FILL COMMAND AND THE PAINT BUCKET TOOL

You'll find the Fill command under Effects on the Main menu bar, or you can use the keyboard shortcut to open the Fill dialog box quickly by holding the **Command-F** (Mac) or **Ctrl-F** (Windows) keys. If you aren't working with a clone at the moment, the dialog box shows the Pattern fill option by default. If you are working with a clone (Chapter 8 will fill you in on all the details of cloning), Fill replaces the Pattern option with the Clone Source option. Figure 3.12 shows the two different phases of the Fill dialog box.

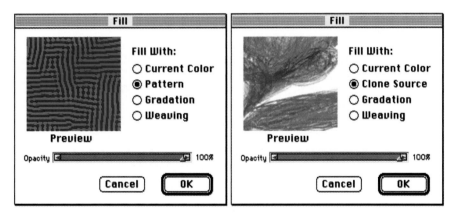

FIGURE 3.12 THE FILL DIALOG BOX SHOWING THE PATTERN OPTION (LEFT) AND THE CLONE SOURCE OPTION (RIGHT).

The Paint Bucket tool is similar to the Fill command with the added benefit of getting instant results as you're moving along. Options for the Paint Bucket are selected on the Controls palette, as Figure 3.13 shows.

```
Controls :Paint Bucket
```
Current Fill

Tolerance ◄ 🔺 ▶ 17

Feather ◀ 🔺 ▶ 207

☒ Anti-Alias

What to Fill
Image ▼

Fill With
Clone Source ▼

FIGURE 3.13 THE CONTROLS PALETTE FOR THE PAINT BUCKET TOOL.

Since there's a crossover of options in the Fill command's dialog box and on the Controls palette when the Paint Bucket tool is chosen, let's review them both at the same time.

❏ **Current Color** fills the area with the primary color you have selected in the Color palette.

❏ **Gradation fills** the area with the colors and gradient type you have chosen in the Grad palette.

❏ **Pattern fills** an area with the pattern you have selected in the Pattern palette. On the Controls palette, the Fill With command uses Clone Source for pattern fills when no clone link is set up.

❏ **Weave fills** an area with the weave you have selected in the Weave palette.

❏ **Clone Source** fills the area with source imagery (Again, see Chapter 8 to unravel this mystery and find out why the subject of cloning keeps coming up!)

GRADIENT, PATTERN, AND WEAVE FILLS

The method of filling for gradients, patterns, or weaves is the same: you click on the palette icon to select the palette for the fill you want to work with. If this takes you to the open drawer (blue bar with green arrow pointing upward), you can select a type visually, by clicking on an icon. Close the drawer (solid blue bar with arrow pointing downward) to select a type or open a new library from the cascading menu list. This closed phase of the drawer also enables you to access the options for fine-tuning your type choice. Once you've made your modifications, you can use either the Fill command or the Paint Bucket tool. Now let's go over each of the palettes in more detail.

GRADIENT FILLS

Painter's gradient feature offers some advanced capabilities to enhance your artwork. This section covers the basics of the Grad palette; refer to Chapter 7 for some special-effects uses.

Click on the **Grad** icon to select the Gradient palette. Open the drawer to choose a type of gradient to work with, or to load a new library (you'll find this item at the bottom of the list), then close the drawer to change to the fine-tuning phase of the Grad palette. Figure 3.14 shows the Grad palette with the drawer closed.

FIGURE 3.14 THE GRAD PALETTE.

At the center of the palette is the preview icon, which will update as you make changes. The red ball on the surrounding ring indicates the angle of the gradient fill, and is easily moved, either by clicking where you want it to be, or dragging it into position.

 The gradient icon with the black-and-white squares on it allows you to apply a gradient fill that uses the currently selected primary and secondary colors.

You may also use the Types icons to change the style of gradation shown in the preview square. To save a gradient you have changed or created, click **Save Grad...** from the Grad pull-down menu, enter a name for the gradient, and click **OK**. If you are using the currently selected colors in the gradient, the icon retains those colors, but it always applies the currently selected colors. Holding down the **Command** (Mac) or **Control** (Windows) key while dragging the red ball changes the radius of a spiral gradient fill.

The six icons at the bottom of the palette control the placement of color in the gradient, which is represented in the color bar right above it. Click on the **Zoom** box in the upper-right corner of the palette window to see these icons, as in Figure 3.14, if they are not already visible.

To capture a gradation from an image and place it in your library, select the gradation using the Rectangular Selection tool. Select the **Capture Gradation** option from the cascading Grad menu. Name your gradation and click **OK**. The gradation is added to the current library. (See Chapter 5 for more information on working with libraries.)

You can create more elaborate gradients with added colors and control of the spread of color. Choose the **Two-Point** type from the Grad palette's type list of preset gradients, and select a primary and a secondary color from the Color palette for your gradation. Next, go to the Grad menu and select **Edit Grad...** to open the dialog box. You'll see a color bar depicting an even distribution between the two colors you have selected. Leave the Linear option unchecked. At the bottom-left and bottom-right corners of the color bar are two triangular points: click on one, then select a different color in the Color palette. You'll see that the color bar automatically updates your choice. Adding more points at the bottom of the bar enables you to add other colors and to adjust where the breaks occur between colors. To add another point, click in the color bar; to remove a point, simply drag it off, either to the left or right side. Drag the points to make more or less subtle transitions between colors.

Figure 3.15 shows the Edit Grad... dialog box as it opens by default and after changes have been made to edit the gradation.

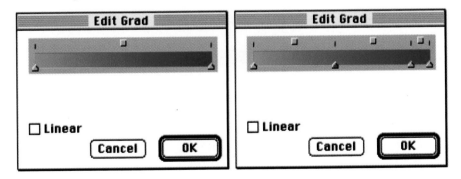

FIGURE 3.15 THE DEFAULT EDIT GRAD DIALOG BOX (LEFT) AND AN ALTERED EDIT GRAD DIALOG BOX (RIGHT).

PATTERN FILLS

 These fills place repeating patterns in your fill area. A pattern is really made up of repeating tiles. The defining tile of the pattern has imagery mapped onto it in such a way that the edges visually connect. You can alter the look of a pattern by changing the tile's size and its vertical or horizontal placement. Select the **Pattern** palette by clicking on its icon in the Art Materials palette, then choose a pattern to work with.

To get a larger view of your pattern as you alter its arrangement, you can select **Check Out Pattern** from the Pattern menu. To create your own pattern, select the area you want to capture using the Rectangular Selection tool and choose **Capture Pattern...** from the Pattern menu. Name and save your pattern to add it to the current library.

WEAVE FILLS

 These fills place a pattern of woven fibers into your fill area. Click on the **Weave** icon on the Art Materials palette to open the Weave palette, choose a type, then close the drawer to customize or create a new weave. Figure 3.16 shows the expanded Weave palette.

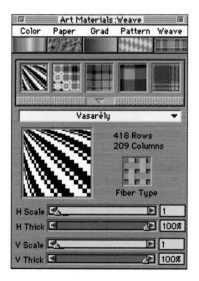

FIGURE 3.16 THE EXPANDED WEAVE PALETTE.

Use the sliders on the expanded palette (click the **Zoom** box if you need to open it more) to change the space between the fibers (scale) and the thickness of the threads. You have separate controls for vertical and horizontal threads.

CHANGING THE COLORS ON A WEAVE

Select **Get Color Set** from the Weave menu to open the color set window for your weave. Choose a new color on the Color palette to replace the unwanted color in the color set, and make sure you have the primary color rectangle selected in the Color palette. Next, click on the color square you want to change and hold down the **Option** (Mac) or **Alt** (Windows) key. To apply this change to your weave, select **Put Color Set** from the Weave menu.

LOCKOUT COLOR AND MASK THRESHOLD

You can further control your fills from spilling over into unwanted areas. Select the particular color you don't want to be painted over from the Color palette, then double-click on the Paint Bucket tool to open the Mask Threshold dialog box. Clicking on **Set** will automatically select the **Lock out color** option and update the preview square. The default setting for this feature is black, to work with cartoon cels.

CARTOON CEL FILLS

Cartoon cel fills sweep color into areas enclosed by line art. If you have any line art that you want to fill with the current color, a gradation, a pattern, a clone source, or a weave, you will use the technique for cartoon cel fills. To draw cartoon cels, you can use any brush that will give you a flat, even line. This includes Pencils, Chalk, Charcoal, Pens, Felt Pens, Crayons, Airbrush, and Artists—brush types you'll find on the Brushes palette. The next chapter, Chapter 4, goes over all your brush choices, but if you're experimenting as you're reading along, the Pens Scratchboard Tool variant is an excellent choice for trying out these features.

After you have drawn the defining lines of your cartoon cel, go to **Select** on the Main menu bar, and choose **Auto Select...**. In the Auto Select dialog box, make sure **Image Luminance** is selected in the pop-up menu, and click **OK**. Next, double-click on the Paint Bucket tool to bring up the Mask Threshold dialog box. Since the lines you create will rarely be perfectly even, increasing the percentage of the Mask Threshold slider will modify the edges of the automatic fill, allowing for that degree of inconsistency in your line work.

Figure 3.17 shows a cartoon cel fill.

FIGURE 3.17 A CARTOON CEL FILL.

PRACTICE EXERCISE

This exercise uses some of the features that control color selection and color fills. The object of this exercise is to gain facility with adding broad areas of color, so you can start to think of how you might apply them to your own work.

1. To start, create a new document that is 4" by 4", 72 pixels per inch, and has white as the paper color. On the Color palette, select a medium blue for the primary color (front rectangle) and a light green for the secondary color (back rectangle). Remember to select the front rectangle again when you're through.

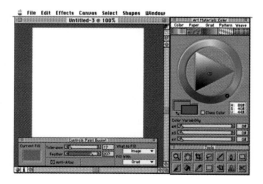

Select the Paint Bucket tool and in the Controls palette, choose **Image** from the What to Fill pop-up menu and **Grad** from the Fill With pop-up menu.

2. On the Grad palette, choose **Two-Point** as the type of gradient from the list of preset choices, then move the red ball on the ring to 45°. Click in your image to fill it with the gradation.

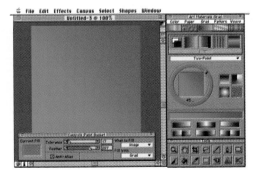

3. Change the primary color to black, then select the **Brush** tool and the **Pens** brush type with the **Fine Point** variant from the Brushes palette. Draw some shapes—it doesn't matter if the shape makes any sense, because we're just using these shapes to see the effect of different fills.

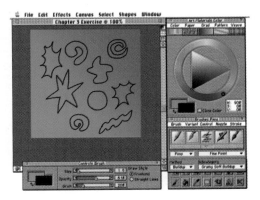

4. With the Paint Bucket tool selected, choose a variety of the different fill types covered in this chapter: gradients, patterns, weaves, clone sources, and current colors. You can use the sliders and options on the palettes to increase or decrease sizes of patterns and weaves, move the "±" HSV sliders on the Color palette to spice up a color fill, and apply different types of gradients.

CHAPTER 4

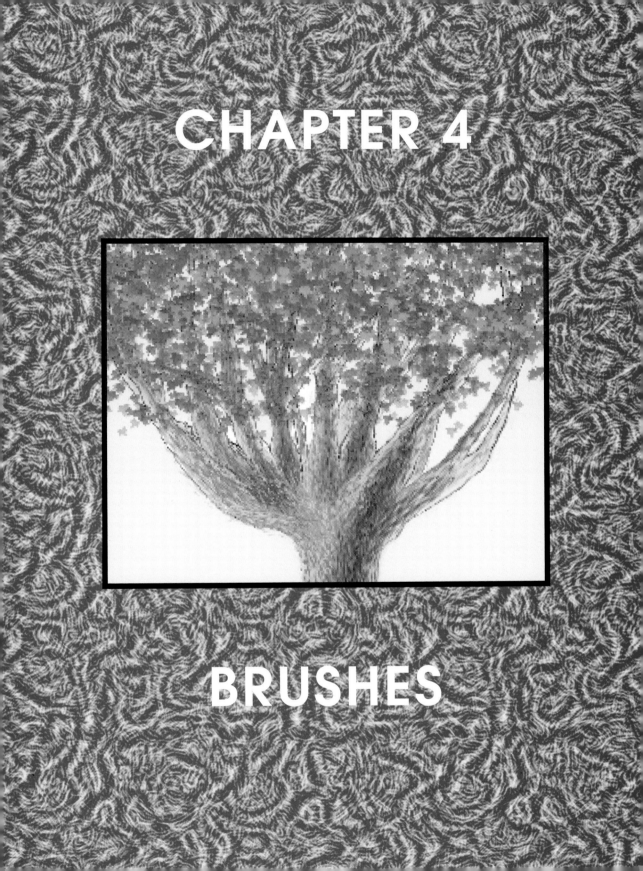

BRUSHES

The core of Painter's magic is its brushes. The sheer range of brush types and the ability to endlessly modify them make the program indispensable for anyone who wants to paint or draw on the computer. The sweep of this array includes brushes that mirror real-world artist's mediums as well as digitally generated brushes that create effects impossible to produce in the real world.

This chapter covers the fundamental workings of the Brushes and Art Materials palettes, and reviews the brush choices Painter has built into the program. As you read along, try out the different brushes to see for yourself how they act, by creating a new document to experiment on. When the page fills up, simply choose **Select: All** and press **Delete** (Mac) or **Backspace** (Windows), to start again. Soon you'll be painting away, changing brushes and colors to your heart's content.

THE BRUSHES PALETTE

To get started, be sure your Brushes palette is displayed. If it's not, select **Brushes** from the Windows menu. Select the Brush tool from the Tools palette, choose a brush from the Brushes palette shown in Figure 4.1, and you're ready to go.

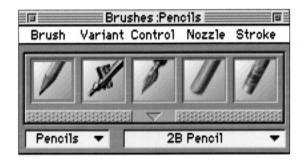

FIGURE 4.1 THE BRUSHES PALETTE WITH THE DRAWER CLOSED.

The Brushes palette displays five choices as icons above a blue horizontal bar with an arrow in its center, indicating that this is a drawer. There are actually

many more choices available, and to reach them, click on the arrow or along the blue bar. This will open the drawer and show the full palette, as you'll see in Figure 4.2.

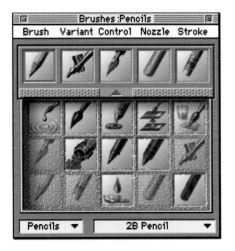

FIGURE 4.2 THE BRUSHES PALETTE WITH THE DRAWER OPEN.

There are as many brush strokes and styles as there are artists creating them. To allow you the ability to paint or draw in a natural way, Painter has built many brush types that correspond to real-world mediums. Each brush type, such as Chalk, Charcoal, Oils, Pencils, and so forth, has variations that emphasize different aspects of that type. For example, Colored Pencils, 2B Pencils, and Sharp Pencils are all Pencils with varying sizes and other attributes that simulate their real-world qualities. You can build upon and change any brush to the nth degree, and the way this is done is the sole subject of Chapter 5. For now, let's get through the basics.

To select a brush type, click on the pop-up menu in the expanded palette drawer: it's the top left menu, below the rows of icons. A cascading menu listing all the types will appear, as shown in Figure 4.3. Drag to your choice and then release the stylus or mouse. Slower computers may exhibit some lag time for some brush types.

FIGURE 4.3 SELECTING A BRUSH TYPE ON THE BRUSHES PALETTE.

The currently selected brush is displayed as an icon on the top row. You will see that it has a red border around it. The icons are displayed in rows on the open palette drawer. As you become more familiar with each brush type's icon, you'll be able to take a shortcut when you want to change the current selection, simply by clicking on the icon itself.

To select a variant of the brush type, click on the top right pop-up menu underneath the icons. Again, click and hold down the stylus or mouse as you scroll through the list, and release when you've made your choice. Figure 4.4 shows the variant pop-up menu.

FIGURE 4.4 THE VARIANT POP-UP MENU.

THE EXPANDED BRUSHES PALETTE

When the Brushes palette is fully expanded, you should see four pop-up menus, as shown in Figure 4.5. If yours isn't already fully expanded, click on the zoom box in the upper-right corner, to see all of your available options. The bottom two pop-up menus are Method and Subcategory.

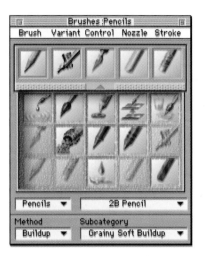

FIGURE 4.5 THE EXPANDED BRUSHES PALETTE.

The Method and Subcategory options determine the nature of the brush stroke and are the key ingredients for customizing your chosen brush type and variant. When you click on the pop-up menus, the lists of choices might seem pretty intimidating, but as you come to understand and use the brushes, you'll see there's a logic to Painter's organization. Think of these choices as further refinements to help you get the style of brush stroke you feel most comfortable using or need at the moment.

Chapter 5 will cover in detail all the features you use to customize your brushes, but it might be helpful with your experimentation to know a couple of points about Method and Subcategory now.

When you begin to paint or draw, the two methods you'll most likely use are Buildup or Cover, found on the Method list. Buildup behaves exactly the way it sounds—each overlaid stroke increases intensity and color. Cover treats each stroke equally and will replace what it overlays with the new stroke and its color, provided that the value, or opacity, of the stroke is the same. You have a lot of leeway with either of these, as the next section explains.

BRUSHES AND THE CONTROLS PALETTE

You can adjust the size of a brush, the opacity of a brush stroke's color, and the amount of the brush stroke interaction with the paper grain by moving the sliders on the Controls palette. Figure 4.6 shows the Controls palette for Brushes.

FIGURE 4.6 THE CONTROLS: BRUSH PALETTE.

The Size slider lets you quickly change the brush size and is a shortcut option that appears on the Brushes: Control palette. But on that palette, there's a Build button you usually need to click for the change to take effect. For this reason, when using the Controls palette Size slider, you must press **Command-B** (Mac) or **Ctrl+B** (Windows) after you make the alteration. Otherwise, an Alert message will appear, prompting you to build the brush.

The general rule of thumb for the Opacity slider is that transparency is to the left; opaqueness is to the right. The value of the Opacity slider merits a little more explanation: simply changing colors on the Color palette by making them lighter or darker won't give you nearly the potential range of colors you can get when working hand-in-hand with the Controls palette. Let's see how this translates for the Buildup and Cover methods.

For Buildup method brushes, moving the slider to the left will keep the color truer to the color you have chosen on the Color palette; moving the slider to the right will increasingly muddy the color.

For Cover method brushes, moving the slider to the left will make the color more transparent, allowing for the overlaying of different colors. Moving the slider to the right will make the coverage more opaque, limiting interaction between colors.

A quick way to change opacities while working is to use your free hand to press the appropriate number key at the top of your keyboard. However, this will make a change only in increments of 10. If, for example, you want the slider to read 47%, you'll have to move the slider in the usual way.

The Grain slider controls the amount of color that penetrates the paper when you use Grainy Method brushes (found under Subcategory, and further explained in Chapter 5). When you move the slider to the right, more grain will show; to the left, less grain shows through.

DRAWING FREEHAND OR WITH STRAIGHT LINES

On the right side of the Controls palette are two choices for the style of your brush strokes. Most of the time you'll be drawing or painting with the Freehand radio button selected, but if you need to draw straight lines, you can do so with almost any brush. You have two options for creating straight lines: you can drag, or you can click. When you click to place points, you can be assured of a perfect connection between your first and last points by pressing **Return** (Mac) or **Enter** (Windows). Please note that when in the Draw Style Straight Line mode, Painter will continue to make line segments any time you click or drag with your mouse or stylus, so temporarily switch back to **Freehand**, then click **Straight Lines** again to make straight lines elsewhere in your image.

PAINTER'S BRUSHES

This section gives an overview of Painter's brushes. Try them out for yourself as you read along. Besides changing brush size, opacity, and textural input, you can mix the different mediums in ways you've never dreamed, like placing chalk over a layer of oils, erasing felt pens, or painting a transparent color into 9 dense and dark color. So, take your rule book out, throw it away, and begin to write a new one.

PENCILS

Pencils react very well to canvas or paper surfaces, as well as to stylus pressure. If you are using a mouse or a standard stylus, you can adjust pencil pressure by moving the Grain slider left (less texture shows) or right (more texture shows) before stroking.

2B Pencil: This is a thin, soft-lead pencil.

500 lb. Pencil: This quarter-ton monster generates fat lines. Very fat.

Colored Pencils: This produces the same effect as traditional colored pencils.

 Sharp Pencil: This is a thin, hard-lead pencil.

 Single-Pixel Scribble: The antithesis of the 500 lb. Pencil, this produces 1-pixel lines—as thin as they get.

 Thick & Thin Pencils: This has the same effect as drawing with both the sharpened tip and the flat edge of pencil lead. It creates lines that vary from thick to thin, depending on the direction in which you are drawing.

ERASER

 You just made a mistake. Not a big deal—just erase it. Painter offers three kinds of erasers, all pressure-sensitive.

 Eraser Variants: These erase right down to the paper color chosen when the document was created. Eraser variants come in five flavors: **Flat Eraser**, **Fat Eraser**, **Medium Eraser**, **Small Eraser**, and **Ultrafine Eraser**.

 Bleach Erasers: Just like undiluted bleach, these variants erase to white, regardless of the paper color. They are available in **Fat Bleach**, **Medium Bleach**, **Small Bleach**, **Ultrafine Bleach**, and **Single Pixel Bleach**.

Eraser Darkeners: A little bit of liberty was taken when these variants erasers were named. Darkeners actually increase the density of the image. Choose from **Fat Darkener**, **Medium Darkener**, **Small Darkener**, and **Ultrafine Darkener**.

WATER

 Use the Water variants to smudge areas and dilute strokes created with any of the other brushes.

 Big Frosty Water: This works like Frosty Water, at about two or three times the width.

Frosty Water: This smears with a harder edge than Just Add Water, while retaining some texture.

 Grainy Water: Use this when you want to retain and work with paper texture. It is also useful for adding texture to smooth areas.

 Just Add Water: This variant smudges with smooth, clean strokes. Be careful, though, because it removes paper grain while it smudges.

 Single-Pixel Water: A tiny smear of water, this is like dragging a wet thread through your image.

 Tiny Frosty Water: This works like Frosty Water, at about half the width.

 Water Rake: This produces the effect of dragging a wet, hard-bristled brush through your image.

 Water Spray: This appears to spray water onto your image, as if you were using an aspirator.

CHALK

 More like traditional pastels than chalk, these brushes are a favorite choice of many artists. You can get some amazing effects when you use the Chalk variants with paper textures and with the Water brushes.

 Artist Pastel Chalk: This variant creates an opaque chalk stroke.

 Large Chalk: This variant works like Artist Pastel Chalk at about twice the width.

Oil Pastel Chalk: This variant slightly smears the stroke beneath it.

 Sharp Chalk: This variant works like Artist Pastel Chalk, at about half the width.

Square Chalk: This variant works like Artist Pastel Chalk, with a sharp, straight edge.

CHARCOAL

 Like traditional charcoal, this brush is great for sketching out your composition, but here you get 16 million colors and no dust. Charcoal produces a more opaque stroke than chalk.

 Default: This is a more textured variant of Charcoal.

 Gritty Charcoal: This produces a rich stroke that varies in width according to the direction of the stroke, as if you were alternating between the flat edge and the point of the charcoal.

 Soft Charcoal: This is a textured variant of this tool, using very soft strokes.

PENS

 The Pens tool contains an incredible assortment of pens, but with no clogging, no ink jars, and no splattering (unless, of course, you want splattering).

 Calligraphy: Fine hand lettering is now a breeze! Select this option for incredible calligraphic strokes.

 Fine Point: This tool works just like a ball point pen.

 Flat Color: A cousin to the 500 lb. Pencil, this lays down an oversized, opaque stroke.

 Leaky Pen: The longer you drag, the bigger the leak. (Careful, you don't want to get this all over your shirt.)

 Pen and Ink: This is a very opaque, smooth stroke.

 Pixel Dust: Not exactly like any pen we've ever used, this tool sprays light dust all over your image.

 Scratchboard Rake: We call this one sgraffito with a cat's claw.

 Scratchboard Tool: This is graffito made fast and easy. For loads of fun, set your paper color to black and scratch away.

 Single Pixel: This is a single-pixel pen, unaffected by stylus pressure.

 Smooth Ink Pen: This variant works like a lettering pen, with greater pressure creating a thicker stroke and less pressure creating a thinner stroke.

IMAGE HOSE

 The Image Hose paints with complete images, not just pigments, spraying the images across your canvas. The Image Hose variants control the way your images—known as Nozzles—flow from the brush. They are grouped according to characteristic.

- *Linear* places images on your canvas in a single line that follows the placement of your cursor.
- *Directional* variants work similarly to Linear variants, placing images on your canvas in single file.
- *Random* places multiple images on your canvas in a random fashion.
- *Sequential* places multiple elements on your canvas in a serial fashion.
- *Size* refers to the amount of spacing between the elements: Small, Medium, and Large.
- *Spray randomly* places images on your canvas as if they had been sprayed on.

The Image Hose variants are covered in greater detail in Chapter 6.

FELT PENS

No, these pressure-sensitive pens won't dry out if you leave the caps off. And they're great for comps, cartoons, and caricatures.

Dirty Marker: This is a much darker and muddier version of the Felt Marker. The nib of this pen is wider for horizontal strokes than for vertical strokes.

Felt Marker: This is a much softer and transparent version of the Felt Pen variants. The nib of this pen is wider for horizontal strokes than for vertical strokes.

Fine-Tip Felt Pens: Press as hard as you want, this narrow pen won't tear your paper.

Medium-Tip Felt Pens: This is about twice the width of the Fine Tip pen, and very opaque.

Single-Pixel Marker: Finer than any pen we've ever used, this marker produces a very thin stroke.

CRAYONS

 When you were little, did you ever beg your parents for one of those great big boxes of crayons—with 96 colors and a sharpener? Well, look what you've got now!

Like their traditional counterparts, these strokes get darker as you layer them; in fact, they can get downright muddy. Press as hard as you want—they won't break.

 Default: Plain and simple, this is a crayon.

 Waxy Crayons: Did you ever put your crayons on the radiator and then try to draw with them? Now you can do that but without getting grounded for a week. Melt away.

AIRBRUSH

 The Airbrush tool lays down gradual tones of color, with a very soft edge to your strokes, as if you were using a traditional airbrush or spray can. As with most other tools, increasing stylus pressure or opacity increases the intensity of your coverage.

 Fat Stroke: This is a thick, soft, semitransparent stroke, good for covering large areas.

 Feather Tip: This lays down soft, thin lines with greater opacity than the Fat Stroke or Thin Stroke variants.

 Single-Pixel Air: This is a very fine Airbrush variant.

 Spatter Airbrush: This is a very textured, transparent, and thick-stroked variant that reacts well to paper texture.

 Thin Stroke: This produces the same coverage as the Fat Stroke, at about one-quarter of the stroke width.

LIQUID

 Most Liquid variants smear more than they paint. You can get effects that range from using oil paints with a palette knife to dragging a wet brush through your image to good old-fashioned finger painting. Use these variants both for applying new paint and adding effects to existing images. To move or smear paint without adding color, reduce your Opacity slider to 0%.

 Coarse Distorto: This is a more textured, less smooth version of the Distorto variant.

 Coarse Smeary Bristles: This is similar to Smeary Bristles, but with a larger stroke and more texture.

 Coarse Smeary Mover: This moves existing paint around with a coarser texture than the Smeary Mover.

 Distorto: This is a very wet, smooth tool that moves, rather than smears, existing paint. Very cool.

 Smeary Bristles: This is a very texture-sensitive and pressure-sensitive tool that smears color from your color palette onto your image.

 Smeary Mover: This is basically the same tool as the Smeary Bristles, but with Opacity set to 0% so that it moves existing paint around rather than adding new paint.

 Thick Oil: This is a very thick, very opaque wet brush loaded with oily paint.

 Tiny Smudge: This is a small, textured smudging tool. The default setting has the Opacity set at 0% so that no color is applied from the Color palette. To add color to this tool, move the Opacity slider to the right.

 Total Oil Brush: This creates a thinner stroke than the Smeary Bristles.

BRUSH

 Although all the tools on the Brushes palette are called "brushes," the more traditional brushes—oil and acrylic brushes—reside here.

 Big Dry Ink: This is a very pressure-sensitive brush that draws separate bristles without looking.

 Big Loaded Oils: This is a broader version of the Loaded Oils brush.

 Big Rough Out: This is a larger, more textured version of the Rough Out variant.

 Big Wet Ink: This variant is highly pressure-sensitive and produces a textural stroke of bristles that remain distinct yet softly blend together.

 Big Wet Oils: This is a broad-stroked brush that mixes its color with the color of the paint beneath it.

 Brushy: This is a multibristled brush that mixes with the colors it is dragged through and runs out of paint at the end of a stroke.

 Camel Hair Brush: This is a softer oil brush than the Oil Paint variant. Slower strokes give the effect of having your bristles closer together; faster strokes spread the bristles. The width of your stroke is reduced with less stylus pressure and increased with greater stylus pressure.

 Coarse Hairs: This is a multibristled, coarse-bristled brush.

 Cover Brush: This is a soft, very slightly textured brush. Increased stylus pressure increases stroke width and opacity.

Digital Sumi: This is a multibristled Sumi brush, with a rakelike effect. Increased stylus pressure increases stroke width.

Fine Brush: This is a multibristled, fine-bristled brush.

 Graduated Brush: This is a thinner oil-type brush that uses two colors, depending on the amount of pressure on your stylus. The colors are taken from the two rectangles on your Color palette. The primary color is selected in the front rectangle; the secondary color is selected in the back rectangle. Greater pressure adds more of your primary color, while less pressure increases your secondary color.

 Hairy Brush: This is your regular bristle brush. The stroke width and grain of this oil-type variant is determined by the amount of pressure placed on your stylus. Less pressure creates thinner strokes with less penetration; more pressure creates thicker strokes with greater penetration. Wait until each stroke is rendered by your computer, or you'll have dots rather than strokes.

 Huge Rough Out: This is a larger, more textured version of the Big Rough Out variant.

 Loaded Oils: This is a multicolored oil brush.

 Oil Paint: This produces an oil-paint effect using a hard-bristled brush. This variant has very hard edges, and the width of your stroke is reduced with less stylus pressure and increased with greater stylus pressure. Grain and Opacity are increased with greater stylus pressure.

 Penetration Brush: This variant works like acrylics and reacts well to surface texture. Slower strokes give the effect of having your bristles closer together; faster strokes spread the bristles.

 Rough Out: So named because it is good for creating rough, textured images. Slower strokes with this dry-brush variant increase the width of your stroke, while faster strokes decrease the width.

 Sable Chisel Tip Water: This is a fine-bristled brush that simulates the smearing effect of painting water onto an image.

Small Loaded Oils: This is a thinner version of the Loaded Oils brush.

Smaller Wash Brush: This is a thin, fine-bristled brush that smears the selected color into the existing paint layer.

Ultrafine Wash Brush: This works just like the Smaller Water Brush, but with a larger number of smaller bristles.

ARTISTS

The Artists variants let you paint using the brush types of the old masters. Increased stylus pressure increases opacity, and faster strokes produce thinner widths.

Auto Van Gogh: This is another way to get Impressionistic results. The Auto Van Gogh variant works using a clone. (Clones are explained in more detail in Chapter 8.)

Flemish Rub: Another take on the Impressionist variant, Flemish Rub smears existing paint to produce an Impressionistic effect on an existing image.

Impressionist: It's easy to emulate the French Impressionists with this tool. Increased opacity adds more color; reduced opacity spreads existing paint.

Piano Keys: This brush variant generates a multicolored stroke that looks like a ribbon of piano keys.

Seurat: This variant gives you the pointillist (dabs of pure color to produce intense color effects) technique developed by Georges Seurat.

Van Gogh: If you use the Impressionist color palette, strokes from this brush give you the multicolored effect used by Vincent Van Gogh. The Van Gogh tool hides underlying strokes, regardless of the Opacity setting. Short strokes work best with this variant. For each stroke, a dotted line is displayed while the image is being rendered. Wait for your computer to completely render the stroke before beginning your next stroke, or you'll have dots rather than lines.

Van Gogh 2: This variant is similar to the Van Gogh variant. The brush strokes appear as you draw them because these strokes require less processing time by your computer (Chapter 5 covers customization of brushes in detail).

CLONERS

Cloner brushes let you take an existing image (usually a scanned photograph) and apply different types of media to them. After you select a default clone setting, Painter provides color information, while you control how the brush strokes are applied. Cloners are covered in detail in Chapter 8, but we'll give you a brief overview of the variants here.

❏ **Chalk Cloner:** This creates the effect of the Artist Pastel Chalk variant.
❏ **Driving Rain Cloner**: This creates an image that looks as if it is being seen through a window in the rain.
❏ **Felt Pen Cloner**: This adds strokes from a felt-tip pen. The darkness (or "dirtiness") of the strokes increases as you lay down more strokes.
❏ **Hairy Cloner**: This produces strokes that emulate the Hairy Brush variant of the brush.
❏ **Hard Oil Cloner**: This lays down hard-edged oil-paint strokes that cover underlying paint.
❏ **Impressionist Cloner**: This paints with the short, multicolored strokes found in the Impressionist variant of the Artist brush.
❏ **Melt Cloner**: This "melts" an image by painting with strokes similar to the Distorto variant of the Liquid brush.
❏ **Oil Brush Cloner**: This paints with oil-paint strokes that cover underlying paint.
❏ **Pencil Sketch Cloner**: This lays down pencil strokes.
❏ **Soft Cloner**: This creates an image in which the edges of the strokes are softer than in the original.
❏ **Straight Cloner**: This recreates the original image.
❏ **Van Gogh Cloner**: This produces strokes that emulate the Van Gogh variant of the Artist brush.

WATER COLOR

The Water Color variants produce beautiful, soft, translucent images. You'll get great results if you use a palette of light pastels. All the Water Color variants react well to surface textures, except for the Wet Eraser.

When you select any Water Color tool, Wet Paint is automatically selected from the Canvas menu. When you do this, you are painting on a layer that "floats" above any existing image you may have on your canvas. When you are through using your water colors, select **Dry** from the Canvas menu. This "dries" your water color layer and sends it to the underlying image layer.

The selection and mask tools do not work on a wet water color layer. To clear a wet layer, select **Dry** from the Canvas menu, select an area, and press the **Delete** key (Mac) or the **Backspace** key (Windows). When you have finished using your Water Color variants, toggle off the Wet Paint selection on the Canvas menu.

Broad Water Brush: This paints with a very wide, translucent stroke that shows some bristle marks.

Diffuse Water: This lays down a concentrated layer of paint with diffused edges. The edges diffuse after the color is laid down, as if it were being absorbed by the paper. Increased stylus pressure increases stroke width and opacity.

Large Simple Water: This is a larger version of the Simple Water variant.

Large Water: This lays down a very wide, lightly colored, translucent layer of paint.

Pure Water Brush: This brush adds water (with no color added) to your image.

Simple Water: This is your basic water color stroke, without bristle marks. Adding layers of colors using this variant produces a smooth, blended effect.

Spatter Water: This variant splatters colored drops of water onto your image, as if you were flicking your brush.

Water Brush Stroke: This is your basic water color stroke, showing bristle marks. Increased stylus pressure increases stroke width. Wait until each stroke is rendered before beginning another stroke.

 Wet Eraser: Use this variant to erase water color strokes on the "floating" layer of wet paint.

Plug-in Brushes

Plug-in brushes are a new feature in Painter 5, and take the possibilities for digital brushes into an altogether different direction. These brushes incorporate special effects with the brush strokes, enabling you to perform such actions as twirling existing imagery, adding glows and texture, and making detailed tonal manipulations, all with the controls you have for any other brush.

There are seven Plug-in Brush types: F/X, Gooey, Layer, Mouse, New Paint Tools, Photo, and Super Cloners. They each have their own libraries of variants and are stored in the New Brushes folder on Painter 5. For instant access to these new brush types, there is a shortcut to the New Brushes palette. If this palette isn't open on your screen, go to Windows on the main menu bar, scroll down to Custom Palette, and select **Shortcut to New Brushes** from the cascading menu. Figure 4.7 shows this palette.

Figure 4.7 The Shortcut to New Brushes palette.

The Pencil icon at the left of the palette enables you to quickly return to Painter's default library of brushes.

The F/X, Gooey, and Photo brushes work by interacting with existing imagery, so you can't use them on a blank canvas. To see how these brush strokes appear, first create a new document that we'll fill with a pattern. Next, open the Art Materials: Pattern palette by clicking on the **Pattern** icon, and select any pattern from the list. Go to **Effects** on the main menu bar and scroll down to **Fill** to open the Fill dialog box, select **Pattern**, and click **OK**.

The Layer, Mouse, and New Paint Tools brushes are an expansion along the lines of Painter's already staggering collection of default brushes, and with one or two exceptions, can be used on an empty canvas. The Super Cloners brush type stands in a category by itself and is covered in detail in Chapter 8.

Once you have loaded one of the Plug-in brushes, the subcategory menu list changes to include some wild effects. Figure 4.8 shows these choices.

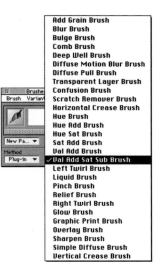

FIGURE 4.8 THE SUBCATEGORY MENU FOR PLUG-IN BRUSHES.

These effects can be used with any of the other brushes in Painter, by choosing **Plug-in** from the Method list.

F/X

As the name implies, the variants of this brush type offer dramatic effects. However, they are highly responsive to the Opacity and Grain settings you input on the Controls palette, so you have a great deal of control over them. You'll be better able to see their effects on images that are either darker or already contain a lot of detail.

Glow: This variant is like painting with a neon light, and like light, the stroke's edges are so diffused that overlapping strokes blend together well.

Fire: This variant literally paints flames onto your image. Use the Controls and Color palettes to determine how many alarms you want your fire to be.

69

Graphic Print: Cut to the chase! As you drag over a color, this variant will grab onto its predominant hue and intensify it. It's only interested in the colors black, white, red, green, blue, cyan, magenta, or yellow. (Subtlety is not its strong point.)

 Confusion: This variant jumbles up pixel information, and the more you overlay these strokes, the more confused the data.

 Bubbles: What does a water drop look like on an image? This variant creates circles that both distort what's underneath and refract light.

GOOEY

 The variants of this brush type distort underlying imagery. Until now, when we wanted to distort areas of imagery we applied a filter, and if we wanted to control placement of the filter's effects, we had to go through the steps of making a selection. Now we can apply the same effects directly, via brush strokes.

 Bulge: This variant will make circular grabs of the image information and distort it outwardly from the center of its circle. If you want to retain recognizable imagery, it's best to use a lower opacity, use shorter strokes, and move slowly.

 Pinch: This variant is somewhat the opposite of the Bulge brush, squeezing imagery together from the center of the brush.

 Horizontal Pinch: This variant will pinch in imagery when you make horizontal strokes, and will bulge out imagery when you make vertical strokes. The higher you set the opacity, the more dramatic the distortion.

 Vertical Pinch: This variant will pinch in imagery when you make vertical strokes, and will bulge out imagery when you make horizontal strokes.

 Left Twirl: This variant creates counterclockwise distortions. Control opacity, brush size, and the length and speed of your stroke if you want to subtly distort your image.

Right Twirl: This variant creates clockwise distortions, and works exactly the same way as its mirror companion, the Left Twirl brush.

Twister: This variant takes the qualities of the Right Twirl brush and pushes them farther.

 Blender: This variant takes the qualities of the Twister variant and drives them over the edge.

 Diffuse Pull: This variant responds to directional pull of your brush stroke, pulling along whatever colors you drag through. Use the Opacity slider to control the degree of color pull.

 Marbling Rake: This variant produces very pretty strokes that drag existing imagery into parallel lines with a marbleized look. Use the Grain slider to alter the effect.

 Runny: This variant throws random distorted strokes on your image as you drag. Both the Opacity and Grain sliders will affect the intensity of the result.

PHOTO

 Now you can apply all kinds of detailed image manipulations on photographs (as well as illustrated art) via the exquisite control of your brush strokes. All these variants work hand in hand with the Opacity and Grain sliders, so for subtle fine-tuning, turn down the volume.

 Dodge: When you want to create separation by lightening an area, you can use this variant. The strokes have very soft edges that blend well with underlying imagery.

 Burn: This variant works by increasing the color's value, darkening the area you paint on.

 Blur: This variant acts just as its name suggests, and its action is deliciously soft.

Diffuse Blur Brush: This variant reveals the directional pull of your brush stroke.

Sharpen: This variant seems to polarize the values of the pixels you drag over, creating a contrasted effect. Be forewarned that a little opacity goes a long way for this one.

Scratch Remover: This variant works by blending adjacent pixel information, allowing you to fill in and effectively remove residual elements on your image, such as dust and lines.

Add Grain: This variant allows you to selectively increase texture on your image via brush strokes, and works hand-in-hand with the paper textures you select in the Paper palette (refer to Chapter 7 for information on paper textures in Painter).

Relief: This variant creates a 3-D effect by accentuating the lights and darks of your imagery as you drag over the area. It reacts to changes on the Opacity and Grain sliders, but its relief effects are independent of paper texture choices.

Comb: This variant is texturally similar to the Relief brush with the added quality of producing directional strokes. Try increasing brush size and lowering opacity to draw textural details on your image.

Overlay: This variant is one of the no-nonsense variety that polarizes existing pixel information, shuffling it neatly into the nearest color hue, so use it with low opacity settings for greater control.

Hue: This variant takes the existing imagery and transposes it to the current color on the Color palette. It works solely with the hue, and will keep the image's existing value and saturation intact.

Hue Add: This variant changes hues, using your current color as the starting point. Working hand in hand with the Grain slider, you can shift hues along the color ring: if the Grain slider is set at 50% or above, the hues move clockwise; below 50%, they move counterclockwise. Very clever design.

Hue Sat: This variant works with the current color in the Color palette and overlays this color on the image. To preserve the existing details, a very low opacity is recommended. (*Sat* = saturation.)

Saturation Add: This variant works with the Grain slider to increase or decrease saturation on your image. Add saturation increasing the slider setting to 50% or more, and decrease saturation with the slider set at 50% or less. Consider the 50% point as the marker starting point for change in either direction.

Value Add: This variant solely works on adjusting the color's value, increasing it when the Grain slider is set at 50% or higher, and decreasing it by moving the slider in the opposite direction.

 Value Add Sat Subtract: This variant works simultaneously on value and saturation, keeping the hue intact. When you want to shift tones in areas with control, this variant would be a good choice. The Grain slider is again utilized: at 50% or higher, there is less saturation and more value (making it lighter); below 50%, your brush strokes increase the saturation and lessen the value (making it darker).

LAYER

 Instead of committing all your brush strokes to the canvas layer, you have the option of painting on a transparent layer that you can later merge with the canvas. The variants of the Layer brush are only a starting point, because almost every one of Painter's default brushes can become a Layer brush by first changing its method to Plug-in and then choosing Transparent Layer Brush from the subcategory menu list. Please note that although you can paint with these brushes directly on the canvas, you won't get the same results.

In Painter parlance, a transparent layer is called a *floater*. Chapter 6 will cover this subject fully, but for now let's create a transparent layer to check out the Brush, Airbrush, and Pen variants of the Layer brush.

With either an existing or a new document open, click on the **Floater** icon on the Objects palette and select **Transparent Layer** from the Floater menu. You're ready to go!

 Brush: This variant is highly pressure-sensitive, and produces a bristly brush stroke that paints as if its fully loaded with color.

 Airbrush: This variant is also very pressure-sensitive, and creates even-toned strokes with very diffuse edges.

 Pen: Also highly pressure-sensitive, this variant can double as a brush by changing its size and opacity settings, producing an even stroke with a soft edge.

MOUSE

Not everyone owns a pressure-sensitive tablet for drawing and painting. Even for those who do, there are times when work has to be done elsewhere, on a computer that doesn't have this luxury attached to it. What to do? Load in the Mouse library and choose a variant that effectively makes your mouse strokes resemble a stylus' brushability.

Dotted: This variant creates dotted lines.

Spirex: This variant is a special effects brush that distorts underlying imagery. Adjusting the Opacity slider will control the degree of the interaction.

Ink Pen: This variant draws clean lines that vary with the speed and direction of your stroke.

Line Tool: This variant draws consistently even strokes, so if you use the hatching method to sketch in form or if straight lines are needed, this would be a good choice.

Scratchy: This variant randomly deposits varying amounts of paint as you drag the mouse, resulting in a more spontaneous feeling to your brush stroke.

Brush Dab: This variant is a larger, softer version of the Scratchy brush.

Rubber Stamp: This variant lets you copy existing imagery and place it elsewhere. Simply click in the area you want to grab, hold down the **Control** (Mac) or **Shift** (Windows) key (you'll briefly see a little number 1, indicating the point of origin), let go, then draw it in the new area.

Single Pixel: This variant draws very fine lines for those times when only a one-pixel stroke will do.

Impressionist: This variant is just like the Artists' Impressionist variant, relying on directional input to create the stroke's appearance.

Calligraphy: This variant is also identical to its namesake, the Pen's Calligraphy variant, and draws as if ink were flowing from a flat-edged nib.

NEW PAINT TOOLS

 This group of variants are an addition to Painter's array of brushes that mirror traditional artists' mediums, with the added quality of interacting with the underlying imagery. They are all highly responsive to changes you input on the Controls palette.

 Palette Knife: This variant acts as a dauber, blending and pushing existing colors together.

 Dry: This variant's daubing action makes only light contact with the canvas, blending and pulling existing colors together.

 Sargent: This variant both pulls along existing color and adds color. You can control this effect by adjusting the Grain slider and Opacity sliders, for blending and coloring, respectively.

 Big Wet Luscious: This variant feels just like oil paints that are mixed with exactly the right amount of linseed oil and turpentine, allowing you to wash in colors with tremendous control. Highly interactive, this stroke works with underlying color and beautifully reveals the direction of added color, depending upon Grain and Opacity input factors.

 Big Wet Turpentine: This variant's default Opacity setting is 0%. It acts as true turpentine does, thinning and smearing existing color. Any increase of opacity introduces the current color.

SUPER CLONERS

This group of brushes perform an altogether different set of actions that form a dynamic part of the Painter landscape. For this reason, they are covered separately, in Chapter 8: Cloning. There you'll find a thorough description of what Super Cloners brushes are and how to use them.

PRACTICE EXERCISE

This exercise introduces you to the world of Painter's brushes and will help you get a feel for the brushes in conjunction with the Controls palette's sliders.

Trees come in all shapes and sizes, leaving any drawing or painting of one wide open to interpretation, so that's what we'll draw in this beginning exercise.

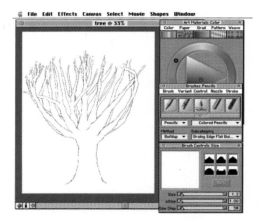

1. To start, create a new document that is 6.5" wide by 8" high, has a resolution of 150 pixels per inch, and has white as the paper color.

   Select the **Pencils** brush type and the **Colored Pencils** variant. For the subcategory, choose **Grainy Edge Flat Buildup**, then lower the Opacity slider to **30%**. Pick a medium brown color on the Color palette, and begin sketching out the trunk and the branches. You're going to be painting in more and more detail, so keep it loose at this stage. If you find you want to clean up or re-draw some lines, switch to the **Eraser** brush type and the **Medium Eraser** variant.

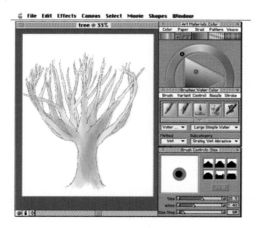

2. Now it's time to paint: select the **Large Simple Water** variant of the Water Color brush. Change the opacity to **20%** and make the brush a little larger—**35.5%**. Start filling in areas, scaling down the brush size as you move up into the branches. Switch to the **Simple Water** variant when you get to the smaller areas. Use a variety of light colors, perhaps changing color every time you change size or opacity.

   Don't worry about straying outside of your sketched lines. With the Simple Water variant selected, choose **Wet Remove Density** from the sub-

category list, set the opacity to **100%**, and remove the color you don't want. When you're through, go to **Canvas** on the main menu bar, and select **Wet Paint** to uncheck it and effectively dry the watercolors into the canvas.

3. In this step we'll add a light gradient fill to the background. Select the **Magic Wand** tool on the Tools palette and click on the white background to generate a quick selection. If some areas in the tangle of branches are missed that's okay, because they'll get covered with leaves later on. Next, choose a light blue on the Color palette as your primary (current) color, then click on the back  rectangle to make it the active recipient for a lighter blue color. Click on the front rectangle again, and open the Gradient (Grad) palette by selecting its icon. Choose **Two-Point** as the gradient type from the palette's menu list, and move the red ball to the top of the ring. Open the Fill dialog box, found under the Effects menu, set the opacity slider to **20%**, and click **OK**. Go under the Select menu and choose **None** to clear the selection before continuing on to the next step.

4. With the added background color, the tree needs some more definition, so we'll paint in some color. Select the **Small Loaded Oils** variant of the Brush method, with **Grainy Soft Cover** as the subcategory. Lower the opacity to **30%** for greater control, and starting with the upper, smaller branches, roughly fill in some color detail. For the wider branches, switch to the **Loaded Oils** variant and 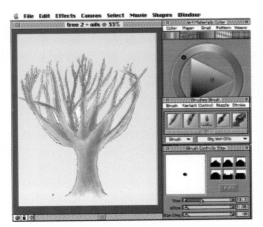 **Grainy Soft Cover** as the subcategory. Lower the opacity to **29%** and con-

tinue to paint in more light and dark color detail. For the trunk, increase the brush size to **16.3%** and lower the opacity to **6%**.

5. Now we'll finish the tree with more color and a lot of textural detail by using a brush that can do both: choose the **Flemish Rub** variant of the **Artists** brush. Change the opacity to **60%** and leave the default settings on the Brushes palette for now. Keep picking different colors on the Color palette and changing brush sizes as you need to, painting in most of the detail on the trunk and lower

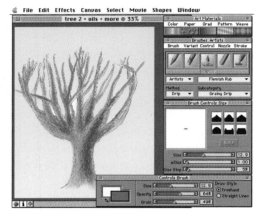

branches. Remember that this variant's appearance reflects the direction of your stroke, so use this quality to embellish your drawing.

As a finishing touch, switch to the Cover method so you can lay in light colors in areas that became too dark, and vice versa.

6. The last step is place some greenery on the tree and under it. First, select the **Image Hose** brush and the **Small Random Spray** variant, then go to the Nozzle menu on the Brushes palette, and select **Nozzles…**. To create leaves we'll work with the **English Ivy** nozzle, modifying its appearance by scaling down its size to **26%** and lowering the opacity to **60%**. Spray in the leaves and as you build, accentuate some

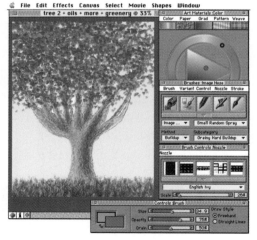

areas by increasing the opacity. You can introduce additional color into your nozzle's spray by selecting a secondary color (back rectangle) and moving the Grain slider left. For the ground, select **Grass** from the list of nozzles, scale down its size to **42%**, lower its opacity to **60%**, and spray in the foreground. For grass that is further back, reduce the size to **25%** and the opacity to **40%**.

CHAPTER 5

CUSTOMIZING BRUSHES

If, after reading Chapter 4, you thought you had plenty of brushes to work with, you're in for a nice surprise. So far, the brushes we've covered are the library of preset, default brushes Fractal Design kindly created to make our lives simpler. But they didn't stop there: they generously included all the digital gadgetry that went into the creation of the Painter library of brushes, so that we can come up with our own variants and even create our own brush types from scratch.

You can modify brushes in almost any way imaginable. Start by deciding what kind of stroke or effect you want to make and what you're going to use it for. Then, set about making the adjustments, editing and refining until you create something that works for you: that's the beauty of digital controls.

CUSTOMIZING BRUSH BEHAVIOR

There are two main places where you will make changes to an existing brush or build a totally new brush. The first area is the Method and the Subcategory properties, which we touched on briefly in Chapter 4. These two pop-up menus are found at the bottom of the expanded Brushes palette. The second area to making modifications is the nine secondary palettes nested under Control on the Brushes palette. Let's start with the first area.

METHOD

Method determines the nature of your brush stroke. Each of the default selections in the Brushes palette already has a method assigned to it that gives it the characteristics of its traditional counterpart.

A brush's method is chosen from the Method and Subcategory pop-up menus on the expanded Brushes palette, shown in Figure 5.1.

Method classifies the basic quality of the brush's stroke, and Subcategory defines the kind of edge and/or general appearance that stroke will have. Strokes are created using a combination of these two properties, the Stroke Method, and the Stroke subcategory, outlined in Table 5.1.

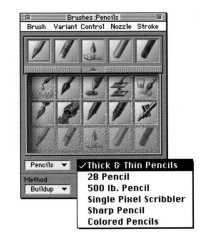

FIGURE 5.1 THE METHOD POP-UP MENU (LEFT) AND THE SUBCATEGORY POP-UP MENU (RIGHT).

TABLE 5.1 STROKE METHODS AND SUBCATEGORIES

Buildup	The Buildup method makes strokes that get progressively darker as you overlay them. The strokes produced by Felt Pens are an example of this method's behavior.
Cover	The Cover method lays strokes on top of each other, covering what is underneath. The strokes produced by Chalk are an example of this method's behavior.
Eraser	The Eraser method holds several options: it can erase, bleach, darken, or smear the colors underneath. The variants included with the Dodge and Burn brushes are examples of this method's behavior.
Drip	The Drip method makes strokes that pull up the underlying color, creating a distorted look. The strokes produced by the Liquid variants are an example of this method's behavior.
Mask (Cover)	The Mask method paints a mask layer directly on the image. Use any brush you like to create truly painterly masks for image editing.
Cloning	The Cloning method lets you replicate an image or part of an image, either on the original document or in a new file. The actions of the Cloner brushes are examples of this method's behavior.

TABLE 5.1 STROKE METHODS AND SUBCATEGORIES (CONTINUED)

Wet	The Wet method works in Painter's Wet layer. The strokes produced by the Water Color brush are an example of this method's behavior.
Plug-In	The Plug-in method adds digital special effects capabilities to any brush. The options range from the subtle ability to selectively add grain with your brushstrokes, to the more dramatic effect of creating a glow.
FLAT	*Flat* creates hard-edged brush strokes.
SOFT	*Soft* produces smooth, anti-aliased brush strokes.
GRAINY	*Grainy* creates brush strokes that interact with the paper texture.
HARD	*Hard* created rough-edged brush strokes.
EDGE	*Edge* produces strokes with a dense, gritty edge.
VARIABLE	*Variable* creates strokes that start with more transparency.

Now, decide what you want in a stroke and choose the method and subcategory that best achieve that goal. It's like ordering from a menu in a family-style restaurant: you choose one option from Column A (Method), and one or more from Column B (Subcategory).

For example, in Figure 5.2, Grainy Hard Buildup gives you strokes that react to the paper texture (Grainy—Column B), have rough edges (Hard—Column B), and eventually build up over each other to muddier, blacker tones (Buildup—Column A). Grainy Soft Cover gives you a paper-grain sensitive (Grainy—Column B), smooth (Soft—Column B) strokes that hide underlying strokes (Cover—Column A). Getting the hang of it?

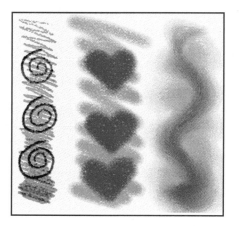

FIGURE 5.2 EXAMPLES OF METHODS.

Let's try one more. Soft Grain Colorize creates paper-grain sensitive (Grainy—Column B), smooth-edged (Soft—Column B) strokes that paint with a mask. "What?" you may say. "Colorize isn't a category." Well, you're right. There are a few items of the Methods pop-up menus that, due to their names, defy our little Column A/Column B system. Let's review them quickly:

- ❏ **Paper Color** (Eraser method) removes paint strokes down to the original paper color.
- ❏ **Paint Remover** (Eraser method) removes paint and replaces it with white.
- ❏ **Paint Thickener** (Eraser method) increases the concentration of a color.
- ❏ **Mask Colorize** (Eraser method) paints within the mask layer from Photoshop and ColorStudio files opened in Painter.
- ❏ **Wet Buildup** (Wet method) produces watery strokes on the Wet Paint layer.
- ❏ **Wet Abrasive** (Wet method) places color over existing paint on the Wet Paint layer.
- ❏ **Wet Remove Density** (Wet method) is the eraser for the Wet Paint Layer.

Got it? Great! Now let's move onto the second major area, and learn how to refine the brush stroke even more.

ADVANCED BRUSH CONTROLS

Advanced options for brushes are found on the Brushes palette under the Control menu. Each one of these options opens a palette that refines a particular property of the brush. These palettes are a mixed bag of controls: not each and every brush is affected by changing all the available controls. However, you can make many subtle modifications to a brush stroke when you learn to know these features, so its worth spending a little time learning something about them.

BRUSH SIZE

The width, tip, and angle of your brush strokes are controlled from the Size palette, the first option found when you click on **Control**. The Brush Control: Size palette is shown in Figure 5.3.

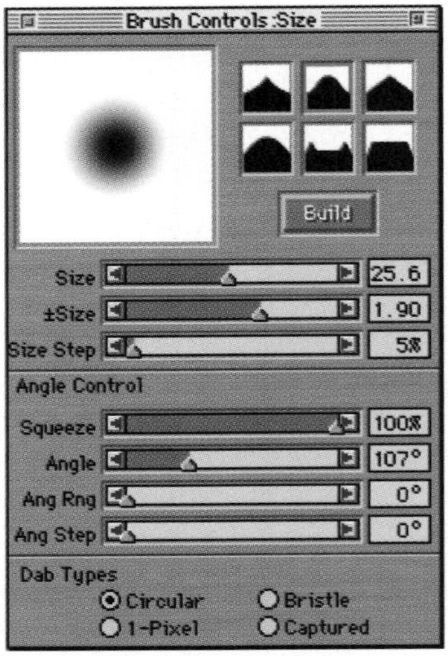

FIGURE 5.3 THE EXPANDED BRUSH CONTROLS: SIZE PALETTE.

❏ *Stroke Contour.* On the upper-right corner of the palette window are six icons, representing six different shapes for the tip of a brush. This feature is concerned with density of color. In general, the first four brush tips' densities spread out progressively. You might choose a contour according to how loose or how tight you want your brush strokes to appear. Please note that not every brush stroke is noticeably altered when you change the contour. Other settings might need to be adjusted, on this palette and in the secondary palettes, before you see a different result.

Pointed: Strokes using this contour provide more color at the center than at the edges of a brush, as with the Sharp Chalk variant.

Medium: This contour produces concentrated color in the center of a stroke, as with the Artist Chalk variant.

Linear: This contour gives strokes with a small area of color in the center of a stroke, as with the Crayons.

Dull: This contour strokes with a moderate amount of color in the center, as with most of the Pencil variants.

Watercolor: Strokes with this contour will pool color at the edges, as with many of the Watercolor brushes.

1-Pixel: Strokes from this nib provide flat color throughout, as with the Calligraphy Pen variant.

❏ *Preview Window*. The preview window in the upper-left portion of the palette displays stroke angle, width (black), and spread of color through a stroke (gray). Clicking on the brush symbol allows you to toggle views of the brush size. One view shows a hard-edged symbol, and the other indicates the spread of color.

❏ *Build*. Click on this button to have Painter build a brush with the options you have selected. You cannot paint with the parameters you chose without first clicking on Build, unless the ± size slider is set to zero.

❏ *Size*. This increases (right) or decreases (left) the width of your brush stroke.

❏ *±Size*. This controls the spread of color through a stroke. Move the slider left to decrease the range of a stroke width, right to increase it. When you move this slider, the black circle in the preview window shows the minimum stroke width, and the gray circle shows the maximum stroke width. This feature is often used with pressure settings.

There are two ways to change the size of your brush. Option one is found on the Controls palette. Simply adjust the Size slider. The second option is through a keyboard command. With your cursor on your image, hold down the **Command-Option** (Mac) or **Ctrl-Alt** (Windows) keys, and drag to create a circle that is smaller or larger than your current brush size. In each case, Painter may prompt you to build the brush, so press the **Build** button on the Size palette, or use the keyboard commands **Command-B** (Mac) or **Ctrl-B** (Windows).

Now let's continue to go through the rest of the Size palette's controls.

❏ *Size Step*. This controls the transition of a stroke from thick to thin and thin to thick. A lower percentage indicates a smoother transition, while a higher percentage provides a much more blunt transition.

❏ *Squeeze*. This determines the roundness of a brush. Moving this slider to the right makes a brush rounder; moving the slider to the left makes the brush more elliptical.

❏ *Angle*. This controls the brush direction of a chosen nib. Use it with the Thinness option, which controls the width of the angle.

❏ *Ang Rng*. This selects the maximum range of angles available in a stroke. Moving this slider to 45° lets a stroke range from 0 to 45°.

❏ *Ang Step*. This controls the number of angles in a brush. A lower setting provides more brush angles, a higher setting provides fewer brush angles.

❏ *Dab Types*. This controls the nature of the brush dab. Briefly, Circular dabs are controlled by the Size palette, Bristle dabs are controlled by the Bristle palette (we'll get there in a minute!), 1-Pixel dabs cannot be resized, and Captured dabs are special brushes that you create (covered later in this chapter) or that have been created by Painter, such as the Chalk brush's Oil Pastel variant. But what is a dab? The following section covers dabs.

DAB SPACING

If you just click once with your stylus or mouse, what you'll see is a dab; when you drag to make a stroke, what you are seeing is actually a series of dabs. The Spacing palette lets you set how close together or far apart you want the dabs to be. This palette also controls the bristle behavior of a brush.

Open the Spacing palette, shown in Figure 5.4, by scrolling down to it under the cascading Control menu.

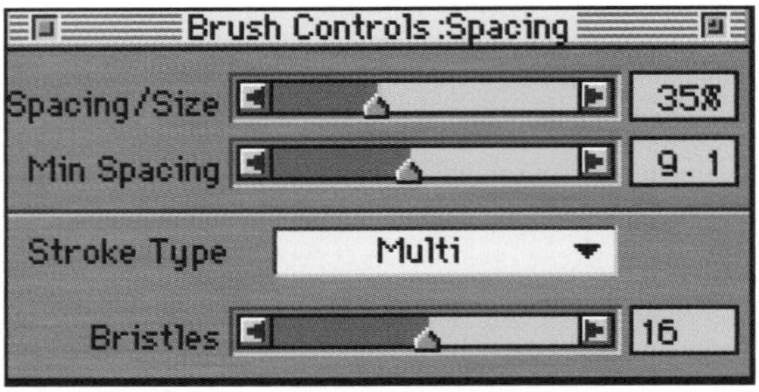

FIGURE 5.4 THE EXPANDED BRUSH CONTROLS: SPACING PALETTE.

Let's take a look at these sliders.

❏ *Spacing/Size.* Controls the space between dabs in a brush stroke. Move the slider left to make the stroke denser and more continuous.
❏ *Min Spacing.* Further refines your "dab factor" by specifying the smallest number of pixels between dabs. Move the slider right to make the dabs further apart.

Real-time, multiple-bristle brushes are brushes that give you incredibly realistic oil-paint and acrylic-paint effects. They are most effective when used with a surface texture.

❏ *Stroke Type.* Determines the bristle behavior of a brush.

Single has one stroke path.
Multi generates brushes that paint with visible bristle marks. Multiple bristles can have more than one color in a stroke.

Rake is a fixed set of evenly spaced strokes that can have more than one color in a stroke.

Hose is a single-stroke type that tells Painter to use the current Image Hose file for a stroke.

❏ *Bristles*. Slider works with the Stroke Type option to control the number of strokes in Multi and Rake strokes. Increasing the number of bristles makes the stroke thicker and appear denser, simply because the more paint a brush can hold, the more paint is deposited on the surface.

RANDOM

It sounds contradictory, but you can program some spontaneity into your brush strokes, paper texture, or clone, with the Random palette. The possibilities include the following:

❏ *Dab Location*. Refers to the pattern of brush "dabs" that form a brush stroke. Moving the slider to the right drops dabs of paint unevenly to either side of the stroke path. No two strokes are the same!

❏ *Clone Location*. Controls factors associated with cloning methods. Increasing **Variability** softens brush strokes and makes them less precise. Decreasing **How Often** generates rougher strokes.

❏ *Random Brush Stroke Grain*. Picks up paper texture at random with each brush stroke, resulting in an nonrepeating version of the paper grain.

❏ *Random Clone Source*. Haphazardly chooses location and source image parts for a wildly distorted effect.

BRISTLE

The Bristle palette, shown in Figure 5.5, lets you customize existing bristle brushes, or build your own, by clicking the **Bristle** radio button on the Size palette. All the default bristle brushes use the Cover method, so that their strokes will cover existing paint.

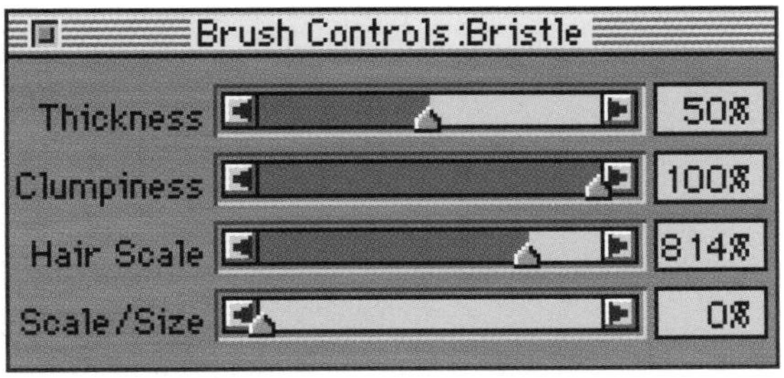

FIGURE 5.5 THE BRUSH CONTROL: BRISTLE PALETTE.

The following are the choices and what they do:

❏ *Thickness.* Controls the width of the bristle set.
❏ *Clumpiness.* Increases (move right) and decreases (move left) the randomness of the bristle path.
❏ *Hair Scale.* Determines the size of the individual bristles.
❏ *Scale/Size.* Increases (move right) and decreases (move left) the variability of bristle size within a stroke.

CLONING

The Cloning palette, shown in Figure 5.6, works hand-in-hand with any cloning action. To activate the Cloning palette you need to choose **Brushes: Control: Cloning,** click on the **Clone Color** option in the Color palette, or choose any cloning brush. Chapter 8 presents all the details of cloning.

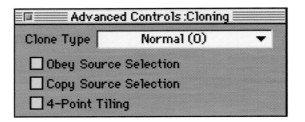

FIGURE 5.6 THE ADVANCED CONTROLS: CLONING PALETTE.

The Clone Type pop-up menu lists nine options, each followed by a number. The types with numbers of 1 or more refer to different kinds of transformations (scaling, rotating, etc.) you can make to your cloned image.

Check **Obey Source Selection** to limit your clone to the selection made in the source document. Use this option when you're transforming your clone.

Check **Copy Source Selection** to include the actual selection made in the source document with your clone in the destination document. This option replicates the original more accurately, including the pixel depth information with the color information.

RAKE

The Rake palette, shown in Figure 5.7, lets you customize existing rake brushes, or build your own, by clicking the Rake option in the Spacing palette. These controls determine the behavior of the bristles in a Rake stroke.

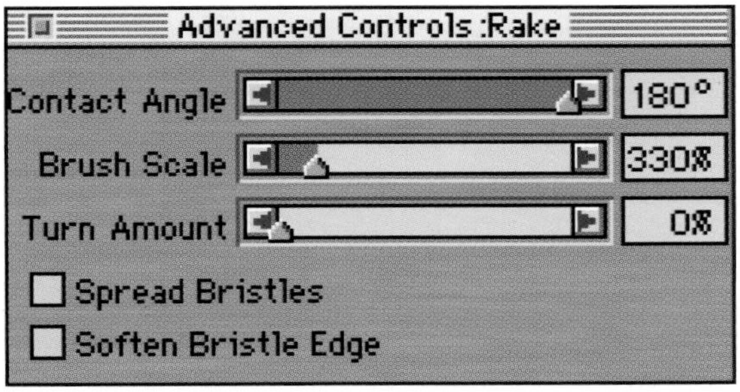

FIGURE 5.7 THE ADVANCED CONTROLS: RAKE PALETTE.

❏ *Contact Angle*. Adjusts how much or how little contact the brush has with the surface. When the slider is at the left, just the tip touches the surface. When the slider is at the right, the entire brush width contacts the surface.

❏ *Brush Scale*. Adjusts the spacing between the individual brushes and affects the stroke size.

❏ *Turn Amount*. Lets you control how the brush stroke will appear at the juncture of a curve or a directional change. When the slider is at the left, the stroke has a continuous tone and stays in constant contact with the surface. Moving the slider to the right makes the edges appear to break up, losing contact with the surface.

❏ *Spread Bristles*. Makes the stroke very pressure-sensitive, alternating the bristles' rake quality with continuous tone. When deselected, the bristles run parallel to each other.

❏ *Soften Bristle Edge*. Drops off the outer bristles to transparent, making the brush stroke softer.

WELL

The Well palette, shown in Figure 5.8, lets you control how much paint is loaded onto the brush and whether the stroke is continuous or fades off as it is drawn. You can also adjust the amount that strokes interplay with each other by depositing more or less paint to let other stroke colors show through.

FIGURE 5.8 THE ADVANCED CONTROLS: WELL PALETTE.

Increase your **Resaturation** value to make the color last longer through a stroke. Increase your **Bleed** value to make colors blend more as you lay your strokes down. Increase your **Dryout** if you want your medium to stay on your brush longer. Set the slider all the way to the right for no dryout. Decreasing this value makes the brush dry out more quickly.

WATER

The Water palette, shown in Figure 5.9, works with Wet method brushes in the Wet Paint layer.

FIGURE 5.9 THE ADVANCED CONTROLS: WATER PALETTE.

Diffusion refers to the edge of the painted stroke and how it interacts with the surface. Moving the slider to the right makes the edge more diffuse, and if you want to diffuse the edge even more, you can select it (see Chapter 6) and press **Shift-D** on your keyboard. You can repeat this keystroke until you arrive at a satisfactory diffusion. **Wet Fringe** increases the amount of pooling on the Wet Paint layer.

SLIDERS

The Sliders palette is a condensed set of controls affecting brush behavior. For the user who only has a mouse to work with, the ensemble approximates settings that make the brush stroke have a more natural feel, as if a pressure-sensitive stylus were being used. The Sliders palette is also used when some sophisticated, special effects are called for, intensifying the stylus' input information. The Sliders palette is shown in Figure 5.10.

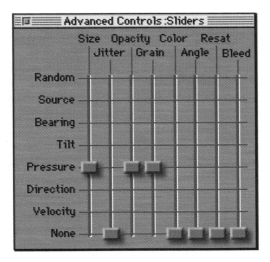

FIGURE 5.10 THE ADVANCED CONTROLS: SLIDERS PALETTE.

Along the top of the Sliders palette are eight items that relate to the brush, and along the left side are eight controls. To get a better idea of how these settings are used, change some brushes and variants and note which settings are used with the defaults. An explanation of the settings follows:

❑ *Size.* Controls how Painter determines brush size.
❑ *Jitter.* Increases or decreases the randomness of a brush stroke.
❑ *Opacity.* Determines how Buildup method brushes operate.
❑ *Grain.* Controls how paper texture is shown through a brush stroke.
❑ *Color.* Allows you to have two-color brush strokes. Choose one of these settings to determine when each color is used.
❑ *Angle.* Adjusts the direction of dabs in a stroke.
❑ *Resaturation.* Controls how much color is retained on a brush through a stroke.
❑ *Bleed.* Determines how colors mix together when you are using a Buildup method brush.

Each of the settings at the left lets you select how you want Painter to determine the preceding options: randomly, according to the source document, bearing and tilt (for tablets that support these features), stylus pressure, stylus direction, stylus velocity (speed), or none (the stroke is unaffected).

CUSTOMIZING THE CONTROLS PALETTE

It's easy to forget that you have all these extra options when you're in the midst of creation—but there is a solution to this problem. If you find a particular set of controls works well with a variant, you can add its set to the face of the main Controls palette. To do so, make sure you have the variant selected that works with these controls. Then scroll through the Brushes: Control cascading menu to select Custom Controls. Make your choices and click **OK**. Every time you choose that particular variant, the main Controls palette will have the extra controls on it. To remove the controls, simply return to the Custom Controls dialog box and deselect your choices.

SAVING BRUSHES AND VARIANTS

Now that you've learned how to customize brushes, you'll need to know how to save and store them. If you don't save, you'll lose them as soon as you select another brush or variant.

Your options for saving and managing brushes and variants are located under the Brushes: Brush menu and the Brushes: Variant menu. Figure 5.11 shows both.

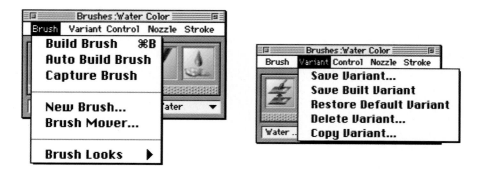

FIGURE 5.11 THE CASCADING BRUSHES: BRUSH (LEFT) AND BRUSHES: VARIANT (RIGHT) MENUS.

SAVING NEW BRUSHES

It's also easy to create a whole new brush category. Of course, you'll want to create a picture to appear alongside the existing icons on the Brushes palette, so first draw a small picture (or use an image that can be imported into

Painter). Next, select a square portion of the picture with the Rectangular Selection tool. With your selection active ("marching ants"), choose **New Brush** from the cascading Brush menu. A dialog box will appear, prompting you to name the new brush. After you click **OK**, look on the Brush palette: your newly created brush will be the last option in the row of icons, and also in the Brush Type pop-up menu. Now that you have a new brush, you can start making some variants for it.

SAVING AND DELETING VARIANTS

To save a brush you've customized, select **Save Variant**... from the cascading Brushes: Variant menu. Then enter a brush name in the Save As field of the Save Variant dialog box. You can select Save Current Colors if you want to include the primary and secondary colors currently selected on the Color palette. Click **OK**, and now you'll see the new brush listed under the Variant pop-up menu on the Brush palette.

To save a customized brush built from a default brush's variant, select **Save Built Variant**. You won't be prompted to name the new brush variant: the name stays the same. If you want to revert the variant back to its default settings, select **Restore Default Variant**, and it will be done automatically.

Because saving variants can be cumbersome in terms of memory, you may want to clean house once in a while. If you're through with a variant and want to remove it, select **Delete Variant**... from the cascading Variant menu. A dialog box will appear asking you if you really want to delete it. Replying **Yes** deletes the variant, and **No** preserves it.

SAVING A CAPTURED BRUSH

The Capture Brush option on the Brush menu enables you to save shapes you've created and build them into brushes, so that you can then paint with them. For example, if you wanted to have a group of bubbles for an underwater illustration, you could draw several circles in different sizes, capture them, then paint away. Here's how: make your drawing, select it with the Rectangular Selection tool, and choose **Capture Brush**. Next, adjust the size to fine-tune it, and click on **Build** when you're done. To keep this new brush, save it as described above.

MANAGING YOUR NEW BRUSHES AND VARIANTS

The ability to create variants is one of the features that makes working with Painter such a joy. If you find you're taking advantage of this option often, it is advisable that you do a bit of organizing with your brushes and their variants to keep things under control.

Painter saves its resources (paper textures, scripts, etc.) in libraries. Each library can hold up to 32 variants. To make everything run more smoothly, and to help you keep track of your new brushes and variants, you can organize them into new libraries. All the actions related to libraries take place in the Movers dialog box, and all the Movers dialog boxes are identical. Figure 5.12 shows the Brush Mover dialog box.

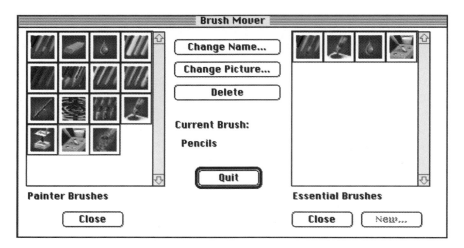

FIGURE 5.12 THE BRUSH MOVER DIALOG BOX.

The left side of the dialog box contains the source library; the right side contains the destination library. First, you'll create a new library by clicking **New** and provide a name when prompted to do so. Next, you'll move items from the source library into the destination library. Make sure the source library is the one you want; if it isn't, click the **Close** button underneath, and when it changes to Open, locate the library you want.

Now you're ready to build your new library. Simply select each item and drag it across into the destination library. Once you've moved the brushes and variants into their new library, you can remove the originals from the source library by selecting them and pressing **Delete.** To rename an item, select it, press **Change Name**, and enter the new name in the dialog box that appears.

If you want to change the icon, first have another picture selected, as described earlier in this chapter, then open the Brush Mover and select the icon you want to change. Press **Change Picture** and you'll be prompted to give the go-ahead.

PRACTICE EXERCISE

This exercise uses the Brushes: Control Well and Brushes: Water palettes. The object of this exercise is to create brush strokes that blend together and become transparent at the end of each stroke. If you were painting the sun, it might have such qualities, so we'll use that as our illustration.

1. To start, create a new file that is 4 × 4 inches, 150 pixels per inch, and has white as the paper color.

   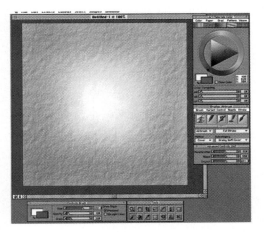

   In the paper palette, choose the **Hand Made** paper texture from Painter's Paper Textures library. Next, choose the Fat Stroke variant of the Airbrush and increase its size to about 122.4. Go to the Brushes: Controls cascading menu and select the **Well** palette. Move the sliders so that they are all roughly in the middle: Resaturation—50%, Bleed—55%, and Dryout—241.7.

2. Now add some background. Create strokes that begin at the outer edge and end in the center. Leave the center clear for the sun, which comes next.

   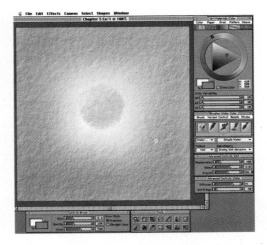

3. When you've finished painting in the "sky," change to the Broad Water Brush variant to begin painting the sun. Move the controls on the Well palette so that they read roughly as: Resaturation—37%, Bleed—87%, and Dryout at its default (changing it doesn't show a result). Draw the main circle depicting the sun.

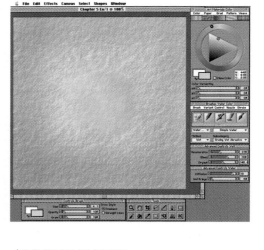

4. Now come the rays: we're after soft, diffused rays that bleed into each other. Choose the **Simple Water** variant. Change the sliders on the Well palette to read as follows: Resaturation—37%, Bleed—70%, and Dryout—148.4%. Open the Water palette under the Brushes: Control menu. Move the Diffusion slider to 14 and Wet Fringe to 6%.

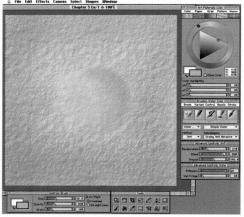

Paint in outward strokes, and adjust colors on the Color palette and sliders on the main Controls palette as you go along. In this exercise, a lower opacity might give you more control than intense color. If you go overboard, you can back up by changing the subcategory to Wet Remove Density.

As you progress, experiment with the Resaturation and Bleed sliders to create different effects.

CHAPTER 6

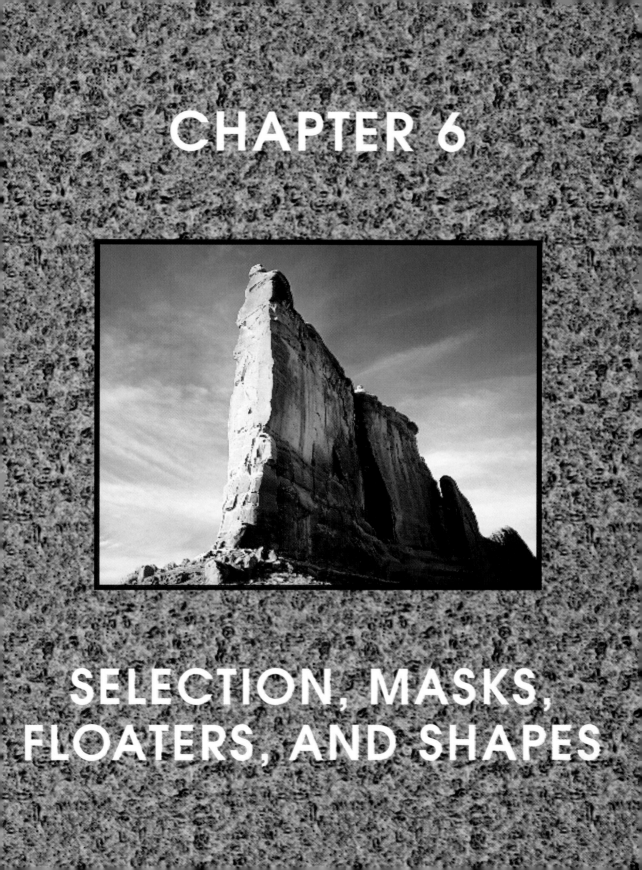

SELECTION, MASKS, FLOATERS, AND SHAPES

Selections, masks, floaters, and shapes isolate areas of your image so you can apply special effects, textures, fills, tonal adjustments, drop shadows, text—and of course, brush strokes.

Painter employs two methods for isolating imagery: selections and masks. *Selections* are vector-based, and use outlines to delineate the area that is being protected on the image. *Masks* are made on an 8-bit layer that has 256 levels of opacity. This gives you the option of having more information to work with, so that your isolated areas can be as precise as you need them to be. Floaters and shapes also isolate areas, as objects that float above the canvas layer. Floaters are pixel-based objects and *shapes* are vector-based, which means they are created differently, but they are treated similarly in that each occupies a separate layer as it is created, making it easy to move, manipulate, and edit them. Floaters are mainly used to composite images, be they photographic or illustrated, while shapes are more often used as a design element.

This chapter covers the fundamentals of selections, masks, floaters, and shapes, and also includes handling text in Painter and the Image Hose, since text is added to an image as a shape, and the Image Hose uses floaters when it sprays images from its nozzle.

SELECTIONS

The selections tools and their functions are clear-cut, and once you get the hang of them, they'll become second nature. If you're already familiar with the selection tools in Photoshop, you'll encounter few surprises here other than orienting yourself to Painter's interface.

CREATING SELECTIONS

Selections are made to protect the areas you don't want to apply changes to, as well as to hone in on the area you do want to work with. When you create a selection, you draw an outline that is represented by a closed group of moving dotted lines: this outline is commonly called a *marquee* or "marching ants."

You can create selections in Painter with the Lasso tool, the Rectangular or Oval Selection tool (they share the same space on the Tools palette), the Magic Wand tool, and with two commands found under the Select menu: **Auto Select** and **Color Select**. The Selections tools are covered in Chapter 2, so we'll briefly cover the commands for generating a quick selection. Choose **Auto**

Select from the Select menu to open its dialog box: the pop-up menu offers six options Painter can use as a basis for a mask. Choose **Color Select** from the Select menu to open its dialog box of sliders that will generate a selection based on hue, saturation, and value. Click once in your image to determine the color range you want to select. Move the H, S, and V Extent sliders left to limit the area to be selected. You can drag around your image in the preview window to see how accurate the selection is (it previews as a mask which is represented as a red overlay). Move the H, S, and V Feather sliders left to control how soft the edges of the selection will be. Click **OK** to exit the dialog box, and you'll see the selection marquee. Figure 6.1 shows a sample working of the Color Select dialog box.

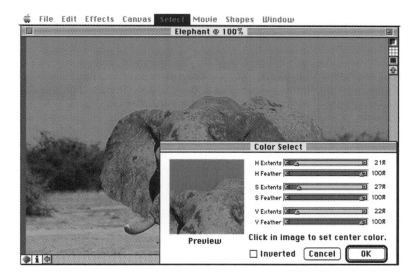

FIGURE 6.1 MOVING THE SLIDERS IN THE COLOR SELECT DIALOG BOX.

WORKING WITH SELECTIONS

Selections protect areas that are either inside or outside their borders. At the lower left corner of the document's window is an icon that pops up when you click on it, giving you the choice to decide which side you're on, so to speak. Such icons are called the Drawing Mode icons, as shown in Figure 6.2.

FIGURE 6.2 THE DRAWING MODE ICONS: DRAW ANYWHERE, DRAW OUTSIDE, AND DRAW INSIDE.

Draw Anywhere means, in effect, that the selection is turned off, no area is isolated, and any change you apply will affect the entire image. Draw Outside means that the selection is protecting areas within its outline from change, and Draw Inside means that you can make changes inside the outline area and that everything outside will remain unaffected.

MANAGING SELECTIONS

The Select menu has several items for managing selections. Reselect enables you to call up the last selection you made, even after you've been busy performing other feats for awhile. Hide Marquee renders the marching ants invisible temporarily, so you can get a clear glimpse of your image, because sometimes their shimmering movement can be distracting. To reveal the selection again, choose **Show Marquee** from the selection menu. Painter stores saved selections in two ways: as masks or in the Selection Portfolio. Save Selection stores your selection as a mask and will appear on the mask list in the Objects: Mask palette (you will find more on masks in the next section of this chapter). For those of you who are familiar with Photoshop, you know that saved selections are stored on the Channels palette; in Painter, they are stored on the Mask palette. When you choose **Save Selection**, a dialog box will open: accept the default choice of **New** from the pop-up menu, click **OK**, and view your newly saved selection in the mask list. Figure 6.3 demonstrates this process.

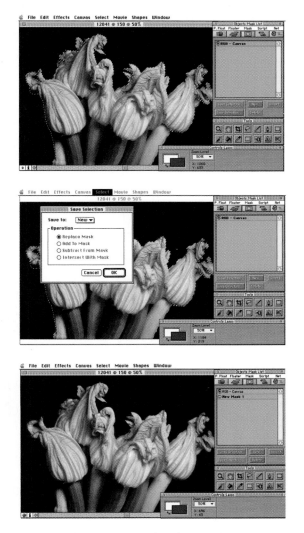

FIGURE 6.3 A SELECTIONS (TOP), SAVING THE SELECTION (CENTER), AND THE STORED SELECTION (BOTTOM).

Images provided courtesy of PhotoDisc, Inc. (1997 PhotoDisc, Inc. All rights reserved.)

When you're ready to use a stored selection, choose **Load Selection** from the Select menu. A dialog box will appear with a pop-up menu listing all the masks: select the one you want, click **OK**, and it will automatically appear on your document. The other way to save a selection is to place it in a library.

Choose **Selections Portfolio** under the Select menu to open its palette. Use the Selection Adjuster tool on the Tools palette to click on the selection you want to save, and drag it into the Selections Portfolio palette. This action will bring up the **Save Selection** dialog box, prompting you to name the selection: do so, and click **OK**. The next time you want to use this selection, simply drag it off the Selection Portfolio palette and onto your document.

EDITING SELECTIONS

You can cleverly use your saved selections to build new ones by adding, subtracting, or intersecting then saving them as a mask. First, make your selections and save them, so they'll be stored in the Mask palette. Next, load one selection, then load another, indicating in the Load Selection dialog box which action you want performed. Figure 6.4 gives an example of combining selections.

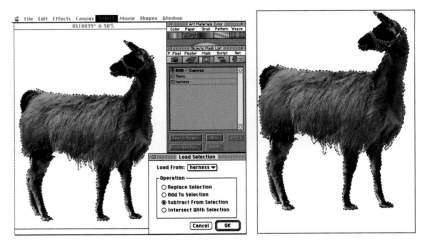

FIGURE 6.4 SUBTRACTING THE *HARNESS* SELECTION FROM THE *LLAMA* SELECTION (LEFT), AND THE RESULTING SELECTION (RIGHT).

Images provided courtesy of PhotoDisc, Inc. (1997 PhotoDisc, Inc. All rights reserved.)

You can also edit path selections by moving, rotating, scaling, and skewing them. Using the Selection Adjuster tool, click on your selection, and handles will appear around it in a rectangular formation. Move your selection by clicking once inside its outline and dragging it into the position you want. To scale, rotate, and skew a mask selection, use the **Transform Selection** command under the Select menu. Still using the Selection Adjuster tool, scale the selection by dragging on any handle; preserve the selection's proportions by holding down the **Shift** key as you drag. To rotate the selection, hold down the **Command** (Mac) or **Ctrl** (Windows) key while dragging a corner handle. To skew the selection drag a side handle while using the same key command, **Command** (Mac) or **Ctrl** (Windows). Figure 6.5 gives you an idea of what these manipulations look like.

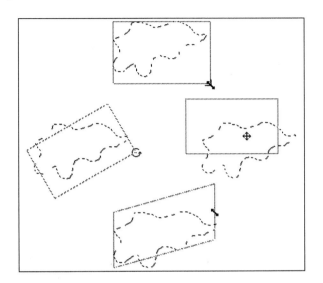

FIGURE 6.5 CLOCKWISE FROM THE TOP—RESIZING, MOVING, SKEWING, AND ROTATING A PATH.

MODIFYING SELECTIONS

The Select menu offers up a number of options to alter your selections once it is created. Some options will bring up a dialog box asking you to enter the pixel width for the area you want to adjust. **Feather...** allows you to control how soft the outline's edges will be. **Modify...** has four choices: you can **widen** or **contract** its outline border, **smooth** out a degree of jaggedness (perhaps caused by imperfect freehand motion), and create a **border**, or parallel selection, that can then be filled with a color, pattern, gradation, or effect. **Stroke Selection** lets you use the outline as an automatic drawing tool, filling it with the current color. Changing drawing modes will affect whether the stroke will fill on the line, inside the line, or outside the line.

MASKS

A mask gives you the freedom to paint in details and protect areas, because you have 256 levels of opacity to work with. When you have created your mask, you need to generate a selection based on the mask. You can then apply brush strokes with any brush, make tonal changes, create certain effects, and add various fills. See the Practice Exercise at the end of this chapter to get an idea of how this feature works. Figure 6.6 shows the Mask palette.

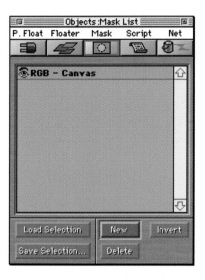

FIGURE 6.6 THE MASK PALETTE.

CREATING MASKS

There are several ways to create masks. The most common one is to save a selection. To start fresh, choose the **New Mask** command under the Mask menu or press the **New** button on the Mask palette, or let Painter generate a mask quickly for you, using the **Auto Mask** or **Color Mask** commands, which you'll also find on the Mask menu list (these work just as the Auto Select and Color select commands do). You can also duplicate an existing mask by choosing **Copy Mask** from the Mask menu list. Figure 6.7 show your choices for creating masks with Mask menu commands.

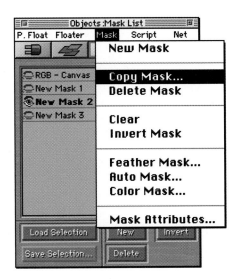

FIGURE 6.7 THE MASK MENU.

Any brush in Painter can be used to create masks. First, choose **New Mask** from the Mask menu to create a new mask layer to paint on. Next, select a brush type and variant, then change its method to **Mask (Cover)**. In the Color palette, drag the circle contained in the triangle to black because you add to your mask with black. When you want to subtract from your mask, drag the circle to white. Any value along the left side of the triangle can be used as well—this is where you create the details (remember the 256 levels of opacity?).

MANAGING MASKS

The Mask palette displays a window containing the mask list. Below the mask list window are several buttons that repeat a few items from the Select menu and the Mask palette menu to provide quicker access to these features. By default, you'll see **RGB-Canvas** at the top of the mask list: this is the composite image layer. As you create new masks, they will appear after this one. Figure 6.8 shows the mask list on the Mask palette.

The Mask palette holds 32 masks on the mask list, so don't be shy about saving selections and creating new masks. To the left of the mask name is an eye icon. When the eye is open, the mask is visible. You can make the mask invisible by clicking on the eye icon, which will close it. Clicking on the mask's name will highlight it in blue, indicating that it is the active mask. If you want to see only the mask, you can click on the RGB-Canvas eye icon to close it, as Figure 6.9 shows.

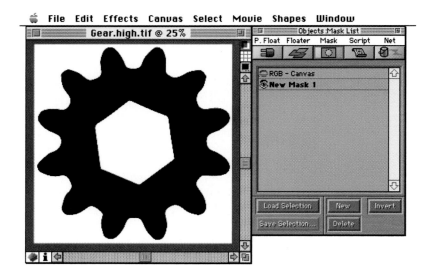

FIGURE 6.8 THE MASK PALETTE'S MASK LIST.

FIGURE 6.9 VIEWING THE MASK LAYER.

Masks appear as a red overlay on your image. To change this color and also its opacity, double-click on the name in the mask list, or select **Mask Attributes** under the Mask menu, to open the Mask Attributes dialog box. The Mask Attributes dialog box is also where masks are re-named. To adjust the feather of a mask's edge, delete a mask, or invert it, you can find these commands on the Mask menu list. Select **Delete Mask** to permanently remove a mask, and select **Clear** to essentially start again with the same mask layer, avoiding the added step of creating a new mask after deleting an old one. Select **Invert Mask** to use the mask's capabilities on the rest of your image. **Delete** and **Invert** also appear as buttons on the palette face for quicker access to these features.

MODIFYING MASKS

When you modify a selection, you are limited by the fact that it exists on a single plane and you must choose either to work inside its outline borders or outside of them. A mask, because of its depth, is much more malleable, allowing you to apply brush strokes and other manipulations to be used as an intermediate step. For example, you can apply a gradation fill onto a mask layer, and then use the mask layer to make a tonal adjustment with a great deal more control that you could by applying it directly on the canvas. Figure 6.10 gives an example of this. On the top is the image as it appeared without any changes. The center example depicts the stage of creating a gradation fill onto the mask layer. Finally, a selection has been loaded, based upon the mask: you can't see its outline because the Hide Marquee was chosen to give you a better view of the change on the image. Tonal adjustments were made using the Brightness/Contrast feature (refer to Chapter 7 for detailed information on working with effects). Please note that the RGB-Canvas layer is highlighted, in order for these changes to take place on the image.

FIGURE 6.10 THE IMAGE BEFORE CHANGES ARE MADE (TOP), CREATION OF THE GRADATION MASK (CENTER), AND THE CHANGED IMAGE (BOTTOM).

You can apply many other effects on the mask layer, though some will be grayed-out, and therefore unavailable.

SAVING MASKS

Masks can be saved and stored in the Selections Portfolio library. First transform the mask you want to save into a path selection by highlighting it and choosing **Load Selection.** Then choose **Select: Transform Selection,** and with the Selection Adjuster tool, click on the selection and drag it into the Selections Portfolio palette.

FLOATERS

Floaters are objects that exist on a layer above the image, or canvas, layer. They allow you flexibility in the creation of your final art, for they can be manipulated in myriad ways.

 To create a floater, you make a selection and then click on it with the Adjuster tool. Selections can be made with any of the methods we've covered so far, including masks when you generate a selection from it by using the Load Selections command. Introducing new imagery via the standard cut, copy, and paste commands is the primary use of floaters and offers endless possibilities: these items are automatically selected when you bring them into your document.

Floaters appear on the Objects: Floater List palette when you create them, as shown in Figure 6.11.

FIGURE 6.11 THE FLOATER LIST PALETTE.

109

There are four types of floaters, and each is represented by an icon.

 Image Floaters are selected imagery that, just like your canvas, are made up of pixels. This affords an incredible bag of tricks for you to use for compositing, especially since they automatically come with a mask layer.

 Reference Floaters are low-resolution versions of Image Floaters that speed up the process of applying transformations. After you scale, rotate, or skew the Reference Floater, it changes back into an Image Floater.

Plug-in Floaters apply dramatic special effects because they interact with underlying imagery, including other floaters.

Shapes are vector-based, and so are limited to manipulations that require no pixels, such as fills, flat painting, and distortions. Text is a prime example of a shape.

To preserve all the floater types in your image so that you can continue to work on the document at a future time, you must save it in the RIFF format. Otherwise, the floaters will be automatically composited into the background. If you want to import your document into Photoshop, save it in the Photoshop format, but be forewarned that Shapes and Plug-in Floaters will be saved as Image Floaters, each appearing on its own layer.

MANAGING FLOATERS

The general rules for working with floaters apply to all four types:

❏ Select a floater by clicking on its name in the Floater List palette or by clicking on it with the Adjuster too in your document. A black-and-yellow border indicates that the floater is selected. You can select additional floaters by holding the **Shift** key as you click.
❏ Deselect a floater by clicking below the listed items in the Floater List palette, or by clicking outside its border with the **Adjuster** tool in your document.
❏ Delete a floater by first selecting it and then pressing the **Delete** button on the Floater List palette or by using the **Delete** (Mac) or **Backspace** (Windows) key.
❏ Rename a floater in the Floater Attributes dialog box, by choosing that command on the Floater menu list, or by double-clicking on the floater name in the Floater List.

❏ Group floaters that are aesthetically linked. To form your group, hold down the **Shift** key and click on each so that the choices are highlighted (bold text against a blue bar), then press the **Group** button on the Floater List palette. Adjustments and commands applied to the group automatically affect every item in it. Rename groups with the Floater Attributes dialog box. You can place additional floaters into an existing group, and take individual floaters out of a group, by clicking on its name and dragging.

❏ Ungroup floaters with the **Ungroup** button on the Floater List palette.

❏ Duplicate a floater by selecting it and holding down the **Option** (Mac) or **Alt** (Windows) key and dragging it to its new location.

❏ Move a floater's position on the list by clicking on its name and dragging it.

❏ **Hide Floater Marquee** will get you a view of your floater minus the black-and-yellow border: this is a command on the Floater menu. When you want to view the border again, select **Show Floater Marquee**.

❏ **Trim** removes the extra space around a floater. You'll find this button on the Floater List palette.

❏ Collapse merges the items in a group into a single floater. You'll find this button on the Floater List palette.

DROPPING FLOATERS

Floaters continue to float above the canvas layer, even when deselected. To merge the floater with the canvas, use the **Drop** button on the Floater List palette. To merge all the floaters in a document at once, use the **Drop All** command on the Floater list.

MANIPULATING FLOATERS

The Controls palette works hand-in-hand with the Adjuster tool to change floaters' opacity, their layering order, and to determine their compositing methods. Figure 6.12 shows the Controls: Adjuster palette.

Controls : Adjuster		
Back Front	Opacity ◀━━━━━━━━━ 100%	W:186 H:165
≪ ≫	Composite Method Default ▼	T:193 B:358 L:608 R:794

FIGURE 6.12 THE CONTROLS: ADJUSTER PALETTE.

By default, floaters appear in the list in order of their creation, with the newest one on top. You can use the buttons at the left of the Controls palette to change the order of their layers.

The **Back** button will move a selected floater to the bottom of the list, while the **Front** button will move an item to the top of the list. The << and >> buttons move selected floaters one layer at a time down or up, respectively. The Opacity slider makes a floater more or less transparent. The transparency of a floater does not affect overlapping floaters.

One of the advantages of creating multiple layers in an image is the ability to make them interact. Composite Methods offer a variety of ways to combine the imagery of separate layers by using hue, saturation, and value information. The Composite Methods are listed in the pop-up menu on the Controls palette. To use a composite method on a single floater, select the floater and apply the effect. If you're compositing it with another floater, make sure to it is under the selected item.

Experience is the best teacher, so by all means, experiment with the compositing methods choices, which are:

- ❏ **Default**: The floating selection covers the image below it.
- ❏ **Gel**: This option tints the image below it using the color of the top image.
- ❏ **Colorize**: This option colorizes the underlying image using the hue and saturation of the top image.
- ❏ **Reverse Out**: This option reverses the colors of the underlying image where the two intersect, going to the complementary color on the color wheel.
- ❏ **Shadow Map**: This option tones down the bright areas of the floater.
- ❏ **Magic Combine**: This option reads the luminance values of both images and combines them.
- ❏ **Pseudocolor**: This option reads the luminance values of a floater and translates them into hues.
- ❏ **Normal**: This option is Photoshop's default method.
- ❏ **Dissolve**: This option blends the floater color with image's color, and as the opacity percentage gets lower, the reason for its name becomes more apparent.
- ❏ **Multiply**: This option intensifies the two layers of color as they are combined, making them darker and less contrasted.
- ❏ **Screen**: This option is the inverse of Multiply, using the combined color information to lighten the area where the two layers of color overlap.
- ❏ **Overlay**: This option keeps the highlights and shadows of the selected floater, but polarizes color information into the pure hue.

❑ **Soft Light**: This option reads the luminance information and lightens or darkens the combined colors, creating a diffused effect.

❑ **Hard Light**: This option reads the luminance information and multiplies or screens the combined colors, creating a harsher effect than Soft Light.

❑ **Darken**: This option reads the light and dark pixel information and conforms overlapping lighter areas to the darker tones.

❑ **Lighten**: This option reads the light and dark pixel information and conforms overlapping darker areas to the lighter tones.

❑ **Difference**: This option determines the brightness values of each selected item, subtracting the less bright layer from the brighter one.

❑ **Hue**: This option reads the underlying image's luminance and saturation values, and combines them with the floater's colors.

❑ **Saturation**: This option reads the underlying image's luminance and hue values, and combines them with the saturation value of the floater's colors.

❑ **Color**: This option reads the underlying image's luminance, and combines it with the hue and saturation of the floater's colors.

❑ **Luminosity**: This option reads the underlying image's hue and saturation values, and combines them with the luminance of the floater's colors.

You can switch compositing methods at any time, until you drop a floater. Each time you change your compositing method, the new method replaces the old one. Figure 6.13 shows the first seven compositing methods.

FIGURE 6.13 CLOCKWISE FROM TOP LEFT, THE FIRST SEVEN COMPOSITING METHODS: DEFAULT, GEL, COLORIZE, REVERSE OUT, SHADOW MAP, MAGIC COMBINE, AND PSEUDOCOLOR.

DROP SHADOWS

Creating drop shadows in Painter is a snap. First select the floater or shape you want to add a shadow to, then go under **Effects** on the main menu bar to **Objects**, and choose **Create a Drop Shadow...** from its cascading menu. This opens the Drop Shadow dialog box, which you see in Figure 6.14.

FIGURE 6.14 THE DROP SHADOW DIALOG BOX.

Click **OK**, and your floater has a shadow, as Figure 6.15 shows.

FIGURE 6.15 A DROP SHADOW.

Images provided courtesy of PhotoDisc, Inc. (1997 PhotoDisc, Inc. All rights reserved.)

Painter reads the shadow as another floater but groups it with the floater above it. Selecting the **Collapse to One Layer** option in the **Drop Shadow** dialog box automatically merges the two.

ALIGNING FLOATERS

Floaters can be lined up horizontally or vertically with the **Align...** command. First, select the floaters you want to arrange, then go under **Effects** on the main menu bar to **Objects** and choose **Align...** from its cascading menu. Figure 6.16 shows the Align Shapes dialog box.

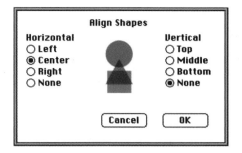

FIGURE 6.16 THE ALIGN SHAPES DIALOG BOX.

TRANSPARENT LAYERS

Floaters are pixel-based, but you are not limited to using only existing imagery for a floater. You can create a transparent layer and paint on it, thereby adding pixel information to a floater from scratch. Choose **Transparent Layer** on the Floater menu to begin. If you know at the outset that you only want to paint on a specific area, you have the additional option of using the Rectangular Selection tool to select the area before you create the transparent layer. To paint, use either one of the Layer brushes or try out the default brushes (there are some that won't work) using the Plug-in method and the Transparent Layer Brush subcategory.

REFERENCE FLOATERS

A *reference floater* is a temporary, low-resolution version of an image floater, and is used only when you need to scale, rotate, or skew an image floater. The value of a reference floater is that it speeds up transformations by virtue of the fact that its information is easier to process. Reference floaters are created either from existing image floaters in your document or by importing imagery from another document. To change an image floater into a reference floater, make sure the image floater is selected, then go under **Effects** on the main menu bar, scroll down to **Orientation**, and choose **Free Transform** from its cascading menu. This feature works on a reference floater just as it does to transform selections: drag a corner handle to scale it (use the **Shift** key to constrain proportions), and use the **Command** (Mac) or **Ctrl** (Windows) key while dragging a corner handle to rotate the image, and a side handle for skewing it. Figure 6.17 shows an example of an image floater and a transformed reference floater.

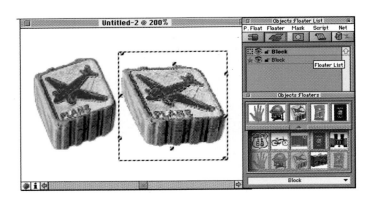

FIGURE 6.17 THE IMAGE FLOATER (LEFT) AND A REFERENCE FLOATER (RIGHT).

When you have completed these operations, change the reference floater back into an image floater by returning to **Effects**, **Orientation**, and choosing the **Commit Transform** command. To bring in imagery from another document, use the **Place...** command, which you'll find under File on the main menu bar. First a dialog box will open asking you to locate and select the correct document, and when you click **OK,** the Place dialog box will open. Move your stylus or mouse over your image to see a rectangular outline that indicates the size of the image you are bringing in. You have several options for positioning your import: you can click a spot in your image, set values in the horizontal and vertical fields within the dialog box, or bypass these and simply click **OK** to center it in you document. This last option is always a safe bet, since it's easy enough to move floaters around using the Adjuster tool. The same commands are used to transform and convert it to an image floater.

PLUG-IN FLOATERS

Plug-in Floaters form a separate category of floaters. Highly interactive with the images underneath them, plug-in floaters combine special effects with the flexibility of floaters. In Painter parlance, they are considered dynamic because they actually leave the underlying image intact while appearing to change it. They are also considered dynamic because their options for manipulation are changeable until it's time to turn them into image floaters and perform other operations. Simply put, they're just a lot of fun.

Plug-in Floaters have different characteristics: some stand alone by creating special effects on a separate layer, some interact with other floaters, and some apply adjustments in an umbrella effect to all the imagery that lies below. You don't create a plug-in floater, you choose one: click on the **Objects:**

P. Float icon to open the P. Float palette, scroll through the pop-up menu, select an option, and click **Apply**. Each plug-in floater has a dialog box with a variety of options for controlling its effect. If you change your mind about using the plug-in floater, you have to click **OK** to exit and then either **Undo** the operation or press the **Delete** (Mac) or **Backspace** (Windows) key to remove it, because the standard Cancel or Close exiting features aren't available in these dialog boxes.

When you create a plug-in floater, its name appears on the Floater List palette, where it is subject to the same rules as the other types of floaters. Double-clicking on its name in the list will re-open its dialog box, so that you can continue to make modifications. When you're satisfied with the plug-in floater's effects, make sure it is selected and choose **Commit** from the P. Float menu. If you don't like the effect, you can clear it and start fresh with the Revert to Original command on the P. Float menu. Be careful not to paint on, apply effects to, or overlap plug-in floaters because these actions will automatically commit the floater. Saving your document in a format other than RIFF will also merge them.

When you want the plug-in to cover only a specific area, use the **Floater Size...** command on the Floater menu to open its dialog box, and enter values in the appropriate fields. Negative numbers will shrink the proportions.

Here are brief descriptions of the Plug-in Floaters:

- ❏ **Brightness/Contrast** applies these tonal adjustments to all the floaters below it, including the canvas layer. You can use the opacity slider, with the Adjuster tool selected, for additional control.
- ❏ **Burn** creates burnt edges on the image floater, complete with jagged edges and varying thickness of discoloration.
- ❏ **Tear** makes the edges look like torn paper.
- ❏ **Bevel World** creates a beveled edge, rendering a 3-D effect on the underlying imagery.
- ❏ **Equalize** automatically adjusts the contrast level to all the imagery that lies beneath it.
- ❏ **Glass Distortion** borrows one of Painter's most luscious effects (see Chapter 7) for use as a floater. This plug-in creates a variety of distortions of underlying imagery, simulating how things appear when viewed through different kinds of glass (or underwater, depending on your point of view).
- ❏ **Kaleidoscope** wildly distorts imagery so that it actually looks as if you're looking at it through a kaleidoscope. The dialog box only asks you to input the pixel size of the plug-in floater, which you then move around on the image to see its effect.

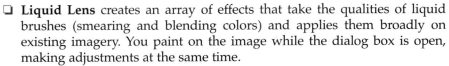
❑ **Liquid Lens** creates an array of effects that take the qualities of liquid brushes (smearing and blending colors) and applies them broadly on existing imagery. You paint on the image while the dialog box is open, making adjustments at the same time.

❑ **Liquid Metal** refracts underlying imagery in ways that liquid or mercury might. Here, too, you paint on the image while the dialog box is open, making adjustments as you need them.

❑ **Posterize** limits the number of colors in underlying imagery, forcing them to conform to the number you allow on its dialog box. This makes the image's colors more graphic.

❑ **Impasto** returns special effects to the roots of Painter, because you input information in its dialog box, click **OK**, and proceed to paint on the selected floater, the canvas layer (when no floaters are selected), or within any selection you create. What makes Impasto unique is that it enables you to paint with brush strokes that have both depth and texture. The strokes are independent of the underlying imagery, so you use the Color palette to select colors.

FLOATER PORTFOLIO

You can save a floater by placing it in a library. Choose **Floater Portfolio** under the Floater menu to open its palette. Use the Adjuster tool on the Tools palette to click on the floater you want to save, and drag it into the Floater Portfolio palette. This action will bring up the Save Selection dialog box, prompting you to name it: do so, and click **OK**. The next time you want to use this floater, simply drag it off the Floater Portfolio palette and onto your document. Figure 6.18 shows the Floater Portfolio palette. As with all libraries in Painter, you customize your saved floaters using the Floater Mover… dialog box. (Refer to Chapter 5 for a sample run-through of how libraries and movers work.)

FIGURE 6.18 THE FLOATER PORTFOLIO PALETTE.

SHAPES

Shapes are vector-based PostScript graphics, like those used in most popular drawing and illustration programs, such as Adobe Illustrator, Macromedia Freehand, and CorelDraw. You can create shapes in Painter or in other applications and then import them into Painter for further work. Painter takes PostScript graphics a step further by breaking past some of the barriers of traditional PostScript to allow for transparency, anti-aliasing (smoothing edges), and the ability to mix vector and bit-mapped images. Even though Painter allows you to create vector-based graphics, you'll probably find it faster to create them in a program dedicated to this type of drawing and then import them into Painter so you can use the program's brushes and tools.

Selected shapes are displayed with thick black-and-yellow lines in a rectangular formation and have handles at the corners and on the sides, as Figure 6.19 shows: this differentiates them from floaters, which don't display handles.

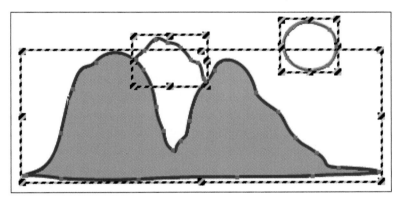

FIGURE 6.19 THREE SELECTED SHAPES.

CREATING SHAPES

Shapes are created with one of the five shape tools: Pen, Quick Curve, Rectangular Shape or Oval Shape, and Text. You can also create shapes by converting a selection, with the **Convert to Shape** command under the Select menu. A third option for creating shapes is to import them from Adobe Illustrator. Under File on the main menu bar, select the **Acquire** command, and locate your file in the dialog box that appears. Another way to open an Illustrator file is through the clipboard, using the standard copy and paste commands. Let's review the tools for creating shapes.

The Pen tool draws with Bezier curves and straight lines. To draw a straight line, click and release the cursor to the point where the line should end and click and release it again. You may continue drawing lines like this to create open and closed shapes. To draw Bezier curves, click where you want your curve to begin. Without releasing the cursor, drag the curve out to create a part of a curve. Release the cursor and continue the click-and-drag process until your curve or shape is complete. If you add a point by mistake, press the **Delete** (Mac) or **Backspace** (Windows) key; Painter removes only the last point added. Don't worry if it's not exactly the way you want it, since you can easily edit Bezier curves by manipulating anchor points and wings.

Anchor points are the points at which a curve begins and ends. *Wings* are the tangential points and lines emanating from each curve that determine the direction of the curve. Click and drag a wing point to change the shape of the curve.

Straight lines and Bezier curves can both be used in the same shape simply by switching between drawing methods while creating that shape. Figure 6.20 shows lines and curves drawn with the Pen tool.

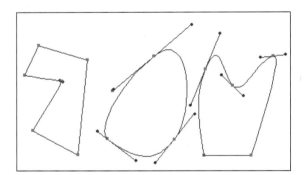

FIGURE 6.20 A STRAIGHT-LINE SHAPE, A BEZIER CURVE SHAPE, AND A MIXED METHOD SHAPE.

If Bezier curves don't work well for you, the Quick Curve tool is your solution. This tool draws shapes as if you were using a traditional pencil. Simply use your stylus or mouse to draw an outline. To create a closed shape, you must end at the same point where you began. As you draw, a dotted line is displayed, and when you release the cursor, the Quick Shape is displayed. If you stop drawing a shape and want to add to it, arbitrarily select an end point and continue to draw your shape from that point. Figure 6.21 shows a shape drawn with the Quick Curve tool.

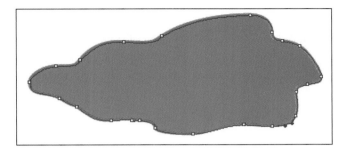

FIGURE 6.21 USING THE QUICK CURVE TOOL.

 Use these tools to create shapes that are either rectangles or ovals. Click or drag to create the rectangle or oval shape; holding down the **Shift** key at the same time will constrain the proportions to a perfect square or circle.

 The Text tool creates shapes from Adobe Type 1 or TrueType fonts. You may apply the same attributes to text as to any other shape object. After selecting the **Text** tool, use the Controls palette to choose a font and a point size. Click where you would like to insert text into your image and begin typing, as in Figure 6.22.

FIGURE 6.22 CREATING TEXT.

MANIPULATING SHAPES

Shapes can be endlessly refined, and you have five tools at your disposal to help resolve any difficulties encountered while constructing them.

Shape Selection manipulates anchor points and wing points. Click on an anchor point to highlight it and proceed with the changes.

 One click of the **Scissors** cuts a segment from a shape.

 Add Point inserts a new anchor point on a curve or line.

 Remove Point deletes an anchor point.

 Convert Point changes anchor points to corner points and corner points to anchor points. Anchor points have wings that lend a curve to the line, whereas corner points are angular.

SELECTING SHAPES

The Shape Selection tool can move several or all points of a shape. To select the points, either click on each one while holding the **Shift** key or drag across the shape to marquee-select the points. To move an entire shape, use the Shape Selection tool to select all of the points or simply drag it with the Floating Adjuster tool.

To join two end points, select them with the Shape Selection tool and choose the **Join Endpoints** command under Shapes on the main menu bar.

COMPOUND SHAPES

The **Compound Shape** option is a bit of a misnomer. Rather than allow you to combine two shapes, it actually lets you use one shape to cut a hole in another. Experiment by creating two shapes and place one over the other, making sure that the top one is smaller so that you'll see the effect. Select both shapes with the Floating Adjuster tool and then select **Make Compound** from the Shapes menu. If you don't like the results, you may convert back at any time by selecting **Release Compound** from the Shapes menu. Figure 6.23 shows a compound shape.

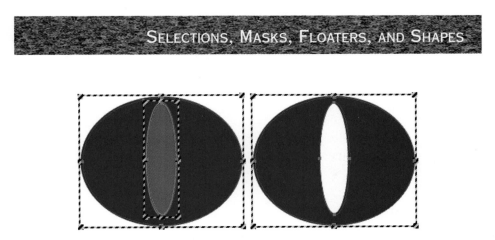

FIGURE 6.23 TWO SHAPES BEFORE AND AFTER MAKING A COMPOUND.

SHAPE ATTRIBUTES

The Shape Attributes dialog box lets you choose how your shapes are displayed. Select the shapes you want to adjust and then press the **Return** (Mac) or **Enter** (Windows) key, or select **Set Shape Attributes...** from the Shapes menu, to open the dialog box, as Figure 6.24 shows.

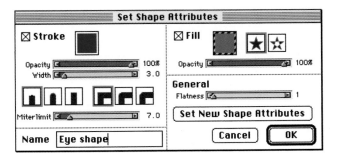

FIGURE 6.24 THE SHAPES ATTRIBUTES DIALOG BOX.

Use the options in this dialog box to adjust the stroke and fill color of the selected shapes. If you would like these attributes to be applied to shapes you create from now on, click on **Set New Shapes Attributes**.

SAVING SHAPE OUTLINES

Painter doesn't have a library to save shapes complete with their attributes, but you can save their outlines in the Selections Portfolio. Convert the shape to a selection and drag it onto the Objects: Selections palette. It is then saved in the currently open Selections library.

CONVERTING SHAPES TO FLOATERS

Another way to save a shape that will preserve most of its attributes is to convert it to a floater. After selecting a shape, choose **Convert to Floater** from the Shapes menu. To save your new floater, drag it onto the Objects: Floaters palette. It is then added to the currently open library.

IMAGE HOSE

 The Image Hose is a brush that paints with images, and each collection of images is called a *nozzle*. Each item in the collection has its own mask that allows you to have the same control over the appearance of the hose images as you have over any floater. In addition to the ten preset nozzles that are supplied with Painter, you can create your own nozzle from any Painter images. Two palettes control the use of the Image Hose: the Brushes palette holds the variants and the Brush Controls: Nozzles palette holds the preset nozzles. Figure 6.25 shows the two palettes.

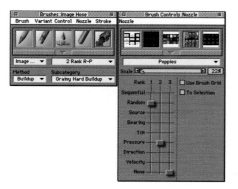

FIGURE 6.25 THE NOZZLE OPTIONS OF THE BRUSHES PALETTE (LEFT) AND THE BRUSH CONTROLS: NOZZLES PALETTE (RIGHT).

USING THE IMAGE HOSE

To use a nozzle, click on the **Nozzle** menu on the Brushes palette and make a selection from the pop-up menu list. Select the **Image Hose** brush on the Brushes palette, choose a variant, and paint away. To add a bit of interest, change the sizes with the Scaling slider on the Nozzles palette. Figure 6.26 shows a sampling of different nozzles.

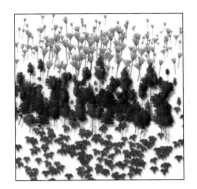

FIGURE 6.26 USING THE IMAGE HOSE.

There are several variants on the Brushes palette.

- ❏ **Size** (Small, Medium and Large) controls the spacing between elements in a Nozzle.
- ❏ **Random Spray** places images in a random (rather than linear) fashion.
- ❏ **Sequential Linear** deposits images in a linear fashion in a particular sequential order.
- ❏ **Random Linear** sprays elements in a linear fashion, but in random order.
- ❏ **Directional** places elements according to the directional specifications on the Size and Spacing palettes. These images are placed in a linear manner.
- ❏ **Small Luminance Cloner** uses the luminance of a cloned image for a nozzle.

Use the Opacity slider on the Controls palette to make a nozzle spray more transparent or opaque. Decreasing the Grain slider adds the currently selected secondary color to the nozzle spray.

CONTROLLING A NOZZLE

You can fine-tune a nozzle using the settings on the Brush Controls Nozzle palette.

- ❏ **Sequential** sprays images from the hose in the order in which you created the nozzle.
- ❏ **Random** sprays image in no particular order.
- ❏ **Source** sprays a nozzle file according to the luminance of a source file.
- ❏ **Tilt** applies a nozzle file based on the tilt of your stylus, providing your stylus supports tilt.

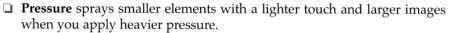

❏ **Pressure** sprays smaller elements with a lighter touch and larger images when you apply heavier pressure.
❏ **Direction** places items according to the direction of your brush stroke.
❏ **Velocity** deposits images according to the speed of your stroke.
❏ **None** applies only the last image in a nozzle file.
❏ **Use Brush Grid** applies a nozzle file based on a grid.
❏ **Add to Mask** places the nozzle spray onto the current mask layer.

CREATING YOUR OWN NOZZLES

You can create a nozzle out of any photographic or painted image in Painter. These images must first be made into floaters before they can be added to a nozzle file. Use the following steps:

1. Open a new image window with these specifications: 500 × 500 pixels and a 75-ppi resolution. Drag any floaters you want to place in the nozzle from the Floater library into this window.
2. Floaters must be individual, not grouped. To ensure this, click the **Collapse** button on the Floater List palette. Click **Trim** to make sure there is no excess space around any floating selection.
3. The order of appearance on the Floater List palette determines the sequence of the images in the nozzle file. Arrange the floaters in the order you want; then select them all and click **Group**. From the Nozzle menu, select **Make Nozzle from Group...** on the Nozzle cascading menu.
4. Painter then creates a new image window with the nozzle elements in it. Select the **Save** option from the File menu and save the image as a RIFF file in the Nozzle folder (inside your Painter 5 folder).

To use your new nozzle, simply load it from the Brush Controls Nozzle palette.

MAKING A NOZZLE FROM A MOVIE

You can take the frames from a movie and turn them into a nozzle file. Open the movie file and select **Make Nozzle from Movie...** from the Nozzle cascading menu.

Painter then creates a new image window with the movie frames in it. Select the **Save** option from the File menu and save the image as a RIFF file in the Nozzle folder (inside your Painter 5 folder). To use your new nozzle, simply load it from the **Nozzle: Load Nozzle...** menu command on the Brush palette.

PRACTICE EXERCISES

FIRST EXERCISE

This exercise introduces you to the sometimes daunting realm of selections and masks. The object of this exercise is to become familiar with some of the mechanics involved in precisely isolating areas so that you can fine-tune you own artwork.

1. To begin, open the file **12034** from the PhotoDisc folder on the CD. We're going to make separate masks for the blue background, for the green tops, and the specks on the strawberries, and for the strawberries. First, select the Magic Wand tool and click the **User Mask** option on the Controls palette, then click on the blue background. To select non-adjacent areas hold the **Control-Shift** (Mac) or **Ctrl-Shift** (Windows) keys while clicking on them.

We've generated this mask just to get us started; now we'll use brushes to finish the drawing. On the Brushes palette, select the **Thin Stroke** variant of the Airbrush and change its method to **Mask (Cover)**. With black as the current color on the Color palette, reduce the Opacity slider on the Controls palette to 10%, and begin to add to the mask where there are gaps.

Observe that the edges between the background and the strawberries are soft, while the mask is not. Try to match this softness with your brush strokes. Zoom in more if you need to. If you go too far in your addition, you can always back up and subtract from your mask by switching the current color to white.

When you are through, double-click on the mask's default name, **Magic Wand Mask**, on the Objects: Mask List palette to open the Mask Attributes dialog box. Type in **Background** to rename it, and click **OK**.

2. Now we'll create a mask for the green areas on the image. First, select the **RGB-Canvas** layer on the Objects: Mask List palette and click the eye icon next to Background to render it invisible. The green tops of the strawberries vary in color and value, so the Lasso tool is a better bet as a selection tool to get the mask underway. Select an area, and **Shift-click** to select the rest. Don't worry about accuracy—we're going to paint in the mask layer and fix it up.

Click the **Save Selection** button on the Mask List palette to change the selection into a mask: accept the defaults in the Save Selection dialog box and click **OK**. Click on the eye icon next to Mask 1 in the Mask List palette to view the mask and make it the active layer.

Proceed to fine-tune this mask as you did with the background mask, and name it **Greenery** when you have finished. If you want to get super-detailed, paint over the little specks on the strawberries with the Feather Tip variant of the Airbrush, increasing its size to 2.8. Reduce the opacity as the specks become more diffuse.

3. Now that you've created these two fabulously accurate masks, you can relax and let the computer do the detail work from here on in. First, select the **RGB-Canvas** layer and make the Greenery mask invisible by clicking on the eye icon to close it. Next, select **Color Mask...** from the Mask menu, click on a strawberry in the image to set the color, and click **OK**. Name the mask **Strawberries**, as you did with the others. The picture for this step shows

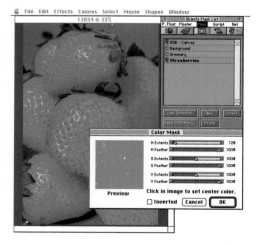

the already masked strawberries with the Color Mask dialog box reopened, so that you can see the slider settings that generated the mask.

4. With the **RGB-Canvas** layer selected and all the mask layers invisible, click **Load Selection** on the Mask List palette and choose **Strawberries** from the pop-up list. Click **OK** to exit the dialog box, then click **Load Selections** to bring it up again. This time, select **Greenery** from the pop-up list and choose the **Subtract from Selection** option.

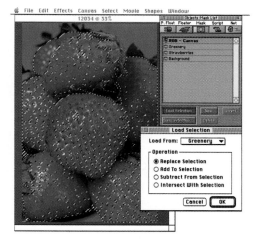

You're now ready to apply color, tonal, textural, and special effects changes to the isolated area.

SECOND EXERCISE

This exercise uses the Text tool. The object of this exercise is to try out some of Painter's features as they relate to text.

1. To begin, create a new file that is 6" wide and 3" high, with a resolution of 72 pixels per inch. Select the Text tool and on the Controls palette, and pick a favorite font from the font pop-up menu. Increase the Point Size

slider to **75** and the Tracking slider to **0.275**. Pick a blue color for your type on the Color palette.

2. Place the cursor on the left side of the document window and type in the word **content**. Open the Floater List palette and making sure all the letters are highlighted, press the **Group** button at the bottom of the palette. Now the letters will be easier to work with.

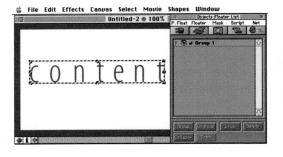

3. Let's place a drop shadow under the seven letters of the word *content*. Go under Effects on the main menu bar, scroll down to **Objects**, and choose **Create a Drop Shadow...** from its cascading menu. The picture for this step shows the type with the drop shadow added and the dialog box reopened so you can see what settings were input to create this particular effect.

4. To apply a fill or effect to the text, make sure the group is selected and choose **Drop and Select** from the Floater menu. As an example, choose **Tonal Control**, **Adjust Colors** from the Effects menu.

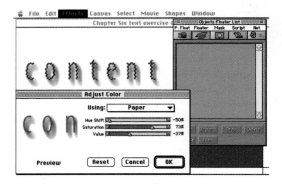

CHAPTER 7

PAPER TEXTURES AND SPECIAL EFFECTS

Painter's ensemble of paper textures and special effects is one of the program's most delightful areas of discovery. The number of default textures Painter supplies are vast, and you have tremendous control over how they'll appear. Best of all, they're so easy to use: you're basically moving sliders or selecting from menus.

Texture is an integral part of an image, though we're not always aware of it on first glance. Painter lets you seamlessly incorporate textures and special effects into your digital creations so that they are on par with any artwork made using traditional media. At the other extreme, textures and effects can be applied to an empty canvas, becoming a piece of art that stands on its own.

Paper textures and effects are applied in two ways as your piece evolves: (1) with the Grain slider on the Controls palette, to let your currently selected paper texture be a part of your brush stroke, and (2) through a variety of commands before, during, and after the creation process. This chapter introduces what's available so you can jump in and explore.

TEXTURES: THE PAPER PALETTE

The Paper palette holds Painter's default texture library, and provides access to the 22 other libraries that come with the program, by selecting the **Load** button at the bottom of the palette's pop-up menu. When you select a paper texture you have the option of changing its appearance by using the Scale slider to increase or decrease its pattern and inverting its texture by clicking the **Invert Grain** option. Figure 7.1 shows these features of the Paper palette.

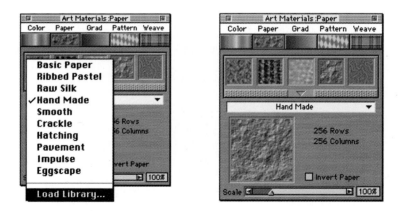

FIGURE 7.1 THE EXTENDED PAPER PALETTE AND ITS POP-UP MENU (LEFT) AND A SELECTED TEXTURE WITH THE PALETTE'S DRAWER CLOSED (RIGHT).

When you select a paper grain by clicking on its icon in the Paper palette, you won't see the background of your image change to that texture. Instead, you'll see the texture reflected in your brush strokes, provided you are using a brush that interacts with paper texture. Any brush that lists **Grainy** in its subcategory menu can bring the quality of texture into your brush strokes. You input to what degree the texture will show through by moving the Grain slider on the Controls palette. Remember, you can always change a brush variant's method and subcategory in order to make it have a textural stroke. Figure 7.2 shows a sampling of how texture appears via a brush stroke.

FIGURE 7.2 CLOCKWISE FROM THE TOP SPATTER AIRBRUSH, LARGE CHALK, DEFAULT CRAYONS, THE BRUSH TYPE'S BIG WET INK, AND THE WATER BRUSH STROKE.

APPLYING PAPER GRAIN TO THE IMAGE AREA

In addition to applying grain to individual strokes, you can apply a three-dimensional paper grain an entire image, or a selected area of it. This works before, during, or after brush strokes have been applied.

On the Paper palette, select the grain you want to use and go ahead and change the size and invert it, if that's your choice. Then go under **Effects** on the main menu bar, and select **Apply Surface Texture...** from the Surface Control cascading menu. The Apply Surface Texture dialog box, shown in Figure 7.3, gives you a preview of how your image will look with the selected texture.

Be sure **Paper** is chosen on the Using pop-up menu, adjust the Amount slider to the percentage of grain you want to apply, and reduce the Shine slider percentage to give the texture a more natural feel. Simply click **OK** and you have instant texture.

If you choose **Image Luminance** in the Using pop-up menu, Painter uses the brightness of the image to decide where to place the texture. Use the Light Controls to have the grain of the paper reflect a light source.

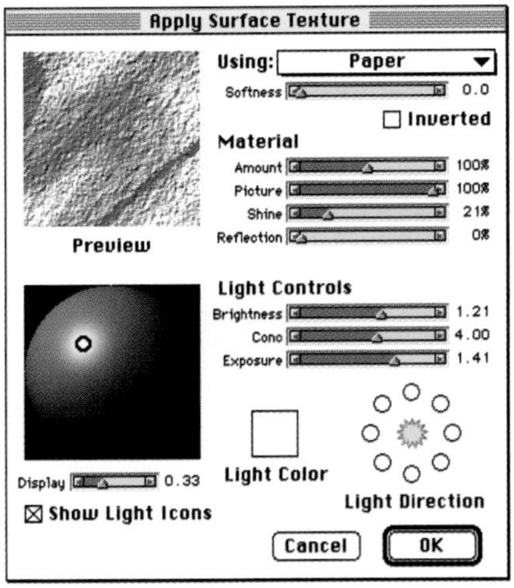

FIGURE 7.3 THE APPLY SURFACE TEXTURE DIALOG BOX.

APPLYING COLOR AND PAPER GRAIN

The **Color Overlay** command, also found under the Surface Control cascading menu, adds both color and texture to the image simultaneously.

In the Color Overlay dialog box (Figure 7.4), select a model. Dye Concentration allows color to be absorbed by the paper, and Hiding Power allows the color to cover the underlying image.

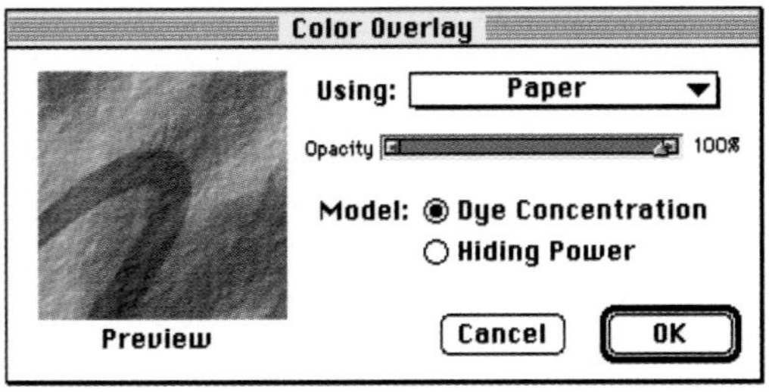

FIGURE 7.4 THE COLOR OVERLAY DIALOG BOX.

Pick a color on the Color palette and adjust the Opacity slider in the dialog box until you see the result you want in the Preview window. Next, select a mode from the Using pop-up menu:

❏ **Uniform Color** overlays a flat, untextured tint.
❏ **Paper** overlays a texture selected in the Paper palette. You can switch papers on the Paper palette while this dialog box is open.
❏ **Image Luminance** generates a texture based on the brightness of an image.
❏ **Original Luminance** texturizes a cloned image based on the brightness of a source image. (See Chapter 8 for more information on cloning.)

CREATING AND EDITING PAPER TEXTURES

Painter's default selection of textures is merely a starting point: the possibilities are endless for you to create your own paper textures, edit existing ones, and organize this new batch into their own libraries for easy access.

REPEATING TEXTURES

To create a new texture based on a preset pattern, select the **Make Paper...** command on the Paper menu to open its dialog box, shown in Figure 7.5.

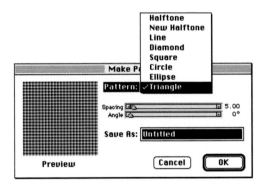

FIGURE 7.5 THE MAKE PAPER DIALOG BOX.

Then follow these steps:

1. Select a pattern type from the Pattern pop-up menu .
2. Increase the value on the Spacing slider to increase the space between each pattern element.
3. Change the value on the Angle slider to change the angle of the pattern.

Your changes are displayed in the Preview window. When you get the result you want, give it a name in the Save As window and click **OK**. This new texture will be added to the end of the paper texture library that is currently open.

CAPTURING A TEXTURE

Let's say you've created a brush stroke (or series of strokes) or have scanned a surface you want to use as an underlying texture for other paintings. Painter makes it easy to incorporate and reuse that texture. First, select the area you want for your texture with the **Rectangular Selection** tool. Next, choose **Capture Texture...** from the Paper menu. In the dialog box, use the **Crossfade** to determine how much of the selected texture will repeat, enter a name for the new texture, and click **OK**. This latest addition will automatically be added to the end of the current paper library.

GENERATING A TEXTURE

Painter gives you the option of creating textures from scratch with **Make Fractal Pattern...** on the Art Materials: Pattern menu list. The options in the dialog box offer a variety of controls to lay down a pattern, which can in turn be used as a textural element in your artwork, or be captured to create a texture for future use.

SURFACE CONTROL

To apply texture to the surface of the image, we've so far covered two commands, both of which you'll find under the Effects: Surface Control cascading menu. This happens because of a slight overlap between special effects and textures in Painter, as you'll soon see. The following section covers some other commands on the list.

LIGHTING

The Lighting feature can add dimension to your image, or a selected part of it. Select **Apply Lighting...** to open its dialog box, shown in Figure 7.6.

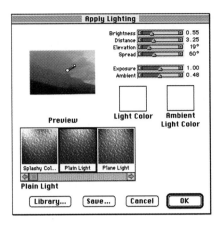

FIGURE 7.6 THE APPLY LIGHTING DIALOG BOX.

First select the type of lighting you want to apply from the scrolling palette at the bottom of the window, then edit the selection with the sliders, viewing the changes in the Preview box until you are satisfied.

To add color to the light source, click on the **Light Color** square. This will open a standard color picker, from which you'll make your choice and click **OK** to continue with the Apply Lighting dialog box. Follow the same steps for the **Ambient Light Color** square.

To adjust the direction of your light source, drag the smaller circle of the lighting icon in the Preview window to place it. To move the icon itself, drag the larger circle into position. To add more icons, and therefore more light sources, click on an existing one and then work with the new one, moving it into place. To delete one, press the **Delete** key (Mac) or **Backspace** key (Windows) on your keyboard.

If you've edited a default light setting and wish to keep it, click on the **Save** button, enter a new name for it, and click **OK**. Your new lighting is now added to the scrolling palette of the current library.

DYE CONCENTRATION

Dye Concentration adjusts the intensity of color in all or a selected part of an image. Here is another place you can add texture to your image. Open the Adjust Dye Concentration dialog box, shown in Figure 7.7, by choosing that command from the Effects: Surface Control menu.

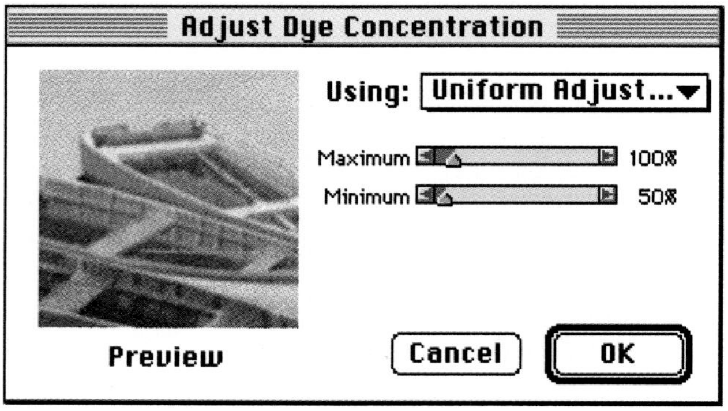

FIGURE 7.7 THE ADJUST DYE CONCENTRATION DIALOG BOX.

Select from the following options in the Using pop-up menu:

❏ **Uniform Adjustment** adjusts only color and does not add texture.
❏ **Paper** adjusts color and adds the Paper palette's currently selected texture, which you can use to switch and preview effects.
❏ **Image Luminance** adjusts the contrast based on the brightness of the image.
❏ **Original Luminance** links a clone based on the brightness of the source image. (Refer to Chapter 8 for more information on cloning).

The Maximum and Minimum sliders adjust the intensity of color in the image. When using the Paper mode, you can increase the texture by lowering the Minimum slider.

IMAGE WARP

Image Warp distorts your image using a linear, cubic, or spherical shape. Click and drag in the Preview window until you get the effect you want.

QUICK WARP

Quick Warp is a souped-up version of Image Warp. You can get all kinds of kaleidoscopic results from this feature. Select the radio button for the shape you want to warp with and click **OK**.

TONAL CONTROL

You'll find the **Tonal Control** cascading menu under **Effects** on the main menu bar. There are several commands here, all of which can be applied to an entire image or a selected or masked portion.

- ❏ **Correct Colors** provides several options for controlling the composite RGB layer and also the separate layers of red, green, and blue.
- ❏ **Adjust Colors** lets you calibrate the HSV values of an image
- ❏ **Adjust Selected Colors** adjusts HSV values based on a central color that is determined by you clicking in the image.
- ❏ **Brightness/Contrast** adjusts the brightness and contrast levels of the image.
- ❏ **Equalize** balances the brightness and contrast settings to optimize them. It finds the lightest and darkest values in an image, averages them, and redistributes the values in between. Use the black-and-white triangle sliders under the histogram (the black mountain-like image) to adjust your image. Adjust the Brightness slider to increase or decrease gamma (midtone values- everything but black and white). You'll see the changes onscreen as you move the sliders. See Figure 7.8 for an example.

FIGURE 7.8 AN IMAGE BEFORE (LEFT) AND AFTER (RIGHT) EQUALIZATION. (*DOCK WITH COLORFUL BOATS* PAINTING COURTESY OF DENNIS ORLANDO.)

- ❏ **Posterize** adjusts the number of color levels an image contains. The lower the number, the more saturated the colors become and the more dramatic the effect will be. Figure 7.9 shows an example.

FIGURE 7.9 AN IMAGE BEFORE (LEFT) AND AFTER (RIGHT) POSTERIZATION.

❑ **Negative** turns your image into a negative, reversing the colors and values, as Figure 7.10 shows.

FIGURE 7.10 AN IMAGE BEFORE (LEFT) AND AFTER (RIGHT) USING THE NEGATIVE OPTION.

ORIENTATION AND DISTORTION

Seasoned imaging software users have come to rely on the computer's ability to perform distortion effects; newcomers will soon see why these manipulations can be indispensable. Under **Effects** on the Main menu bar, select **Orientation** to view its cascading menu with the following items:

❑ **Rotate** turns your image or selected area in increments of 0.1 degrees. Enter the value in the dialog box or drag on a handle to change the position, and click **OK**.

❑ **Scale** changes the dimensions of the image or selected area. Either click and drag on the handles that appear around the image or enter horizontal and vertical values in the dialog box. Click **Constrain Aspect Ratio** to proportionally scale an image. Click **OK** to accept the changes.

❑ **Distort** warps the image in a selected area. Click and drag on the handles that appear around the selection. If you click on the **Better** check box, you get a more accurate distortion, but it takes more time to be rendered. Click **OK** to accept the changes.

❑ **Flip Horizontal** works on an entire image or a selected area.

❑ **Flip Vertical** works on an entire image or a selected area.

FOCUS

The options on the Focus cascading menu allow you to sharpen and blur an image or a selected portion of it.

❑ **Sharpen** increases the contrast of adjacent pixels to increase the clarity of an image. Be careful with this one—you can get some wild results if you over sharpen. Figure 7.11 shows the sharpening of an image.

FIGURE 7.11 AN IMAGE BEFORE AND AFTER SHARPENING.

❑ **Soften** is the opposite of Sharpen and has the same effect as putting a filter on a photographic lens, as Figure 7.12 shows.

FIGURE 7.12 SOFTENING AN IMAGE.

❏ **Super Soften** is a more intense version of Soften.
❏ **Motion Blur** creates the illusion of movement by making an image appear as if you had photographed it while it was moving, as Figure 7.13 shows.

FIGURE 7.13 USING MOTION BLUR.

❏ **Glass Distortion** makes your image appear as though you were viewing it through glass, as in Figure 7.14.

FIGURE 7.14 USING GLASS DISTORTION.

❑ **Camera Motion Blur** is created by dragging in your image, so you'll get different results depending on the speed, length, and directional pull of your stroke, as Figure 7.15 shows.

FIGURE 7.15 AN IMAGE BEFORE (LEFT) AND AFTER (RIGHT) USING CAMERA MOTION. (*SOULS DEPART* PAINTING COURTESY OF KEN KRUG.)

❑ **Depth of Field** reads the brightness values in the image and blurs the darks more, since they appear to be receding. The Maximum slider needs to be higher than the Minimum slider for this to work. Figure 7.16 shows an example of this item.

FIGURE 7.16 AN IMAGE BEFORE (LEFT) AND AFTER (RIGHT) USING DEPTH OF FIELD.

❏ **Zoom Blur** creates a tunnel effect by first clicking in your image to determine the center of the zoom, then adjusting the Amount slider to control the area of the effect, as Figure 7.17 shows.

FIGURE 7.17 AN IMAGE BEFORE (LEFT) AND AFTER (RIGHT) USING ZOOM BLUR.

MORE SPECIAL EFFECTS

The Effects: Esoterica cascading menu holds the wilder set of special effects commands.

❏ **Marbling** turns any image or selection into a marbled masterpiece. Specify the Rake Path, which is the direction of marbling, to get the effects you want. Figure 7.18 shows an example.

FIGURE 7.18 APPLYING MARBLING.

❏ **Blobs** uses either a color or an item on the current clipboard to place floating blobs on an image. Use the Fill Blobs With pop-up menu in the dialog box to choose the current color, paste buffer, or pattern. Blobbed images are great candidates for marbling. Figure 7.19 is a blobbed version of Figure 7.18.

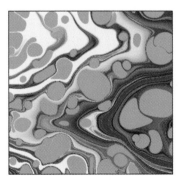

FIGURE 7.19 A BLOBBED IMAGE.

❏ **Grid Paper** adds grid lines to all or part of an image. These lines are editable as if they were applied by painting them on.
❏ **Highpass** lets higher-frequency areas show through while suppressing lower frequency areas. It has the effect of highlighting areas of brightness

and increasing contrast in areas that are lacking contrast, as Figure 7.20 shows.

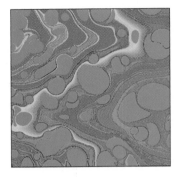

FIGURE 7.20 APPLYING HIGHPASS.

❏ **Auto Clone** and **Auto Van Gogh** are covered in Chapter 8.
❏ **Custom Tile** automatically turns an image into tiles, translating the lighter areas into tiles and the darker areas into grout (the cement that holds tiles in place). Figure 7.21 shows an example of a tiled image.

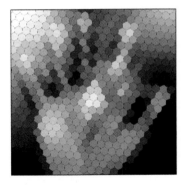

FIGURE 7.21 APPLYING CUSTOM TILE.

❏ **Growth** uses branches to create different patterns, and you can come up with an endless variety of results by playing with the settings in the dialog box. Figure 7.22 shows a sampling of Growth.

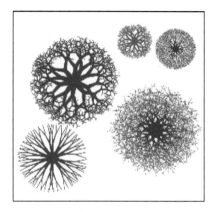

FIGURE 7.22 APPLYING GROWTH.

❏ **Maze** creates a pattern that totally covers the image or the selected portion of it, and is especially useful as a base background or for generating a new pattern or paper texture by capturing a section of it.

❏ **Place Elements** lets you control the area where brush strokes are placed, such as the spray of the Image Hose, which can be a bit tricky to control. Figure 7.23 shows an example of this.

❏ **Pop Art Fill** creates a halftone effect using the information in the image, as Figure 7.24 shows. You pick the particular colors within the dialog box.

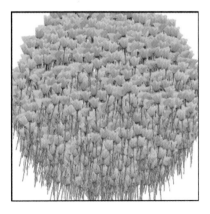

FIGURE 7.23 APPLYING PLACE ELEMENTS.

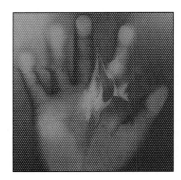

FIGURE 7.24 APPLYING POP ART FILL.

PLUG-INS

You can access third-party plug-ins in Painter, but first you have to locate and choose a folder. Under **Edit** on the Main menu bar, scroll down to **Preferences**, and select **Other Raster Plug-ins** to open its dialog box. Find the proper folder in an application that contains plug-ins, such as Photoshop, then select it and click **OK** to close the dialog box. In order for these plug-ins to be recognized, you'll have to close out of Painter and restart your computer (just this one time, or when you reinstall Painter).

PRACTICE EXERCISE

There are many ways to incorporate the features covered in this chapter into your artwork. This exercise uses a sampling of the Effects menu commands and will help you gain some experience with textures, effects, and distortions.

First we'll create a new document and create a background of sky and earth. Then we'll import a selected portion of another image and apply some changes so it fits in with the background.

1. To begin, create a new file that is 7.25 inches wide and 5.25 inches high with a resolution of 150 pixels per inch. Pick a light blue on the Color palette and choose a texture on the Paper palette. Open the Color Overlay dialog box by selecting that command

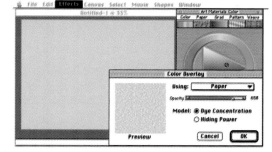

from the Surface Control cascading menu. Choose **Paper** from the Using pop-up menu. Choose the **Dye Concentration** model. Adjust the opacity if you need to, and click **OK**.

2. Now we'll add the ground. Select the **Large Chalk** variant of the Chalk brush, with the **Grainy Soft Cover** sub-category. In the Brush Controls: Size palette, increase the Size slider to **72.5** and the (Size slider to **2.01**. On the Controls palette, decrease the Opacity to **50%** and

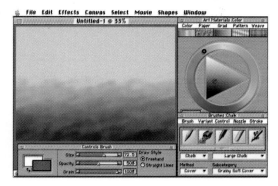

increase the Grain to **100%**. Lay in some earth-toned brush strokes and don't worry if they are crude and overlap, because in the next step we're going to apply an effect to blend the strokes.

3. From the Focus menu, choose **Glass Distortion** to open its dialog box. Select **Paper** from the Using pop-up menu and increase the Amount and Variance sliders until the strokes in the Preview window seem to melt together, then click **OK**.

4. Open the file entitled **0S18025** from the PhotoDisc folder on the 5 CD. This is a photo of a piglet lying down. Select the **Magic Wand** tool and click on the white background to select it, then go under Select and choose **Invert** so that the pig is selected. Next, copy this piglet to the clipboard to import it into the newly created file by selecting **Edit: Copy**.

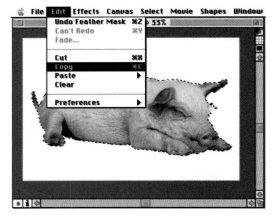

5. Click on the background document to make it active, then choose **Edit: Paste, Normal**. The piglet is now a floater in the new document. Since it needs to be scaled down a bit, select **Orientation** and scroll sown to **Scale...** on its cascading menu. Click on a handle, drag toward the interior of the rectangle to shrink the imagery, and when it looks about right to you, click **OK**.

6. Because it is a photograph, the floater image is sharp compared to the painted background. Let's adjust by blurring the image a bit. Select the **Soften...** command from the Focus menu, adjust the Radius slider to **2.0** in the dialog box, and click **OK**.

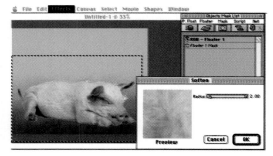

Consider this exercise a starting point: you can use the background and the floater to try out different features, or drop the floater into the background (see Chapter 6 for information on floaters) and continue to apply textures and special effects.

CHAPTER 8

CLONING

To clone in Painter is to perform artistic feats that go beyond mere mechanical replication of imagery. There's more than one method of cloning and the array of tools at your disposal is staggering. Once you get the basics down, you're on your way to creating artwork that is at once derivative and original, something that wholly reflects your personal style.

The range of capabilities the cloning feature allows is extremely flexible and quite sophisticated. You can start with a crisp photograph and turn it into a painting; you can trace an image and take its composition into a new direction, you can make a composite of numerous images; and you can apply transformations such as rotating, scaling, and other distortions.

CLONING AN IMAGE

In order to use any of the cloning tools and effects, you must have open both an original image and a clone. The original, in Painter parlance, is technically known as the *source document*, and the clone is technically referred to as the *destination document*.

It's a snap to make a clone. With the source document open, go to File: Clone, and your image is quickly duplicated. Figure 8.1 shows an image and its clone.

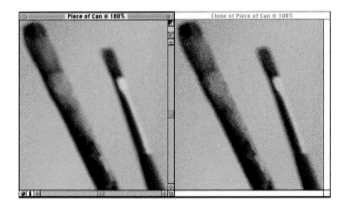

FIGURE 8.1 AN IMAGE AND ITS CLONE. THE SOURCE DOCUMENT IS ON THE LEFT; THE DESTINATION DOCUMENT IS ON THE RIGHT.

Read the names of the documents. On the left is "Piece of Can," and on the right is "Clone of Piece of Can." After you work on this and want to save it, you have the option of naming it as you would any other document.

When you are working with cloned images, you must leave both the source and clone documents open, since the clone is linked to the source.

If you close your source and clone images and open them again at another time, you'll have to reestablish the link between them. To do this, open the two images, go to File: Clone Source, and select the name of the source from the pop-up menu, which lists all the documents that are open. You can use this option to clone on one document from multiple images: just keep designating the Clone Source as you go along to establish the link between the source document and your cloning area.

CLONING METHODS

The basic cloning method creates a copy of an image, duplicating all the pixel information, intact. This kind of clone works well when you want to change the original in a traditionally artistic way, using the Cloning brushes or any brush with the cloning method and applying strokes to the clone.

The second cloning method functions just like Photoshop's Rubber Stamp tool, in which you hold down the Control (Macintosh) or Shift (Windows) key, and click with your stylus or mouse to determine your point of origin, and then paint elsewhere to copy the source information. Painter's feature is distinctive, however, in that you can actually use any brush to alter the source imagery considerably, painting as you clone. Painter calls this method *point-to-point cloning*. If for some reason you're not seeing a crosshair as you work, go to the Edit: Preferences: General dialog box and check **Indicate clone source with crosshairs while cloning**. Figure 8.2 shows how this method works.

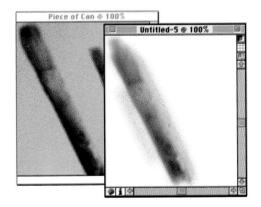

FIGURE 8.2 A SOURCE IMAGE (LEFT) AND A FEW STROKES IN A CLONE USING THE SOFT CLONER BRUSH VARIANT (RIGHT).

The third, and final, cloning method is derived from point-to-point cloning, and actually multiplies that formula. You first plot two to four points in the original, and plot and adjust an equal number of points for the clone, and then paint with a brush to effect some specific transformation. For example, if you want to copy a flower, make it smaller, and turn it slightly so that it differs from the original, you can easily do so with this more advanced cloning method.

In addition to these three distinct ways to clone, there are a few surprises, such as the Auto Clone and Tracing Paper features. The rest of this chapter covers everything you'll need to know.

CLONER BRUSHES

Painter provides a Cloner brush type, but feel free to experiment with all the brushes, as this will really expand your range of possibilities. When you use these brushes, you control the placement and direction of your brush strokes. Remember, you must keep your source image open while working in cloner mode. In the following sections, let's briefly go over the Cloner brush variants.

CLONER BRUSH VARIANTS

Any variant that uses a Grainy subcategory reacts well to the selected paper texture. You may also look at the method as it relates to the variant. (The Cloner brush type uses various methods like Cover, Buildup, and Drip.) As with other brushes, you may use any or all of the customization techniques described in Chapter 5 to adjust Cloner brush variants to your specific needs.

Figure 8.3 shows the source image we are using in these examples.

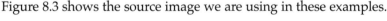
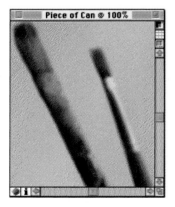

FIGURE 8.3 THE ORIGINAL IMAGE.

The following list describes Cloner brush variants.

- **Chalk Cloner** This variant lays down strokes like the Artist Chalk brush and reacts very well to paper texture.
- **Driving Rain Cloner** This variant clones an image as though it were being viewed through the rain.
- **Felt Pen Cloner** This variant clones an image using felt pen strokes. Like the Felt Pen brushes, strokes from the Felt Pen Cloner build up and get darker as you apply them.
- **Hairy Cloner** This variant clones an image with strokes like the Hairy Brush variant, showing bristle lines and reacting to paper texture.
- **Hard Oil Cloner** This variant clones an image using oil-paint–like strokes with a hard edge. This is a cover brush using a Grainy method, so that it covers underlying strokes and reacts to paper texture. Each time you lay down a stroke, a dotted line is displayed on your image. Wait until the line renders into a stroke before beginning your next stroke, or you won't get the results you want.
- **Impressionist Cloner** This variant clones images with short, multicolored strokes like the Impressionist variant of the Artist brush.
- **Melt Cloner** This variant clones an image using drippy, smeared strokes.
- **Oil Brush Cloner** This variant clones an image using oil-paint–like strokes with a soft edge. Each time you lay down a stroke, a dotted line is displayed on your image. Wait until the line renders into a stroke before beginning your next stroke, or you won't get the results you want.
- **Pencil Sketch Cloner** This variant clones an image, using pencil strokes.
- **Straight Cloner** This variant clones your image without any changes—it exactly reproduces the source image.
- **Soft Cloner** This variant clones an image with soft-edged, airbrushlike strokes.
- **Van Gogh Cloner** This variant clones with multicolored strokes, like the Van Gogh Artist brush variant. You will get better results if you use short strokes. Each time you lay down a stroke, a dotted line is displayed on your image. Wait until the line renders into a stroke before beginning your next stroke, or you won't get the results you want.

AUTO CLONE

If you have already tried some of the Cloner brushes, you may have discovered that it can take a long time to cover a large area. If you want Painter to handle some of the work for you, you can use the Auto Clone feature.

To use this feature, set up your source and destination files and select the brush variant you want to use. You may clone an entire image or select a portion of it. If you are not using a Cloner brush variant, select **Clone Color** on the Color palette so that your brush uses the colors from your source image.

Select **Auto Clone** from the cascading Esoterica menu, found under the Effects menu. Your image is automatically cloned using the selected brush variant, as in Figures 8.4 and 8.5. Painter continues adding paint to your image until you stop the Auto Clone process by clicking anywhere in the image.

FIGURE 8.4 USING AUTO CLONE WITH THE SEURAT VARIANT.

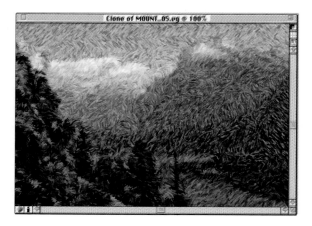

FIGURE 8.5 USING AUTO CLONE WITH THE VAN GOGH VARIANT.

Auto Clone works best with the Driving Rain, Seurat, and Van Gogh variants.

TRACING PAPER

Tracing is an invaluable artist's tool to help bring ideas into workable form. Whether you're creating a comp for an ad, a sketch for an illustration, making detailed selections to use later, or generating frames for an animation, you'll soon find that this feature is practical and easy to use.

To set up your digital tracing paper, have your source image open and clone it. Make the cloned image the active document, and select all of it. Next, press **Delete** (Mac) or the **Backspace** key (Windows), and don't panic when the image disappears—that's what we want. Under Canvas on the Main Menu bar, select **Tracing Paper**, and a ghost of the original image will appear. This ghosted background is the tracing tool, and will not print; it really isn't part of that document.

You can use any brush to trace. You have the additional option of selecting **Clone Color** on the Color palette to pick up colors from the original image. Figure 8.6 shows the original image and the cloned image with Tracing Paper turned on.

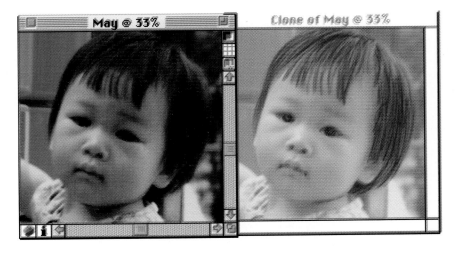

FIGURE 8.6 ORIGINAL (LEFT) AND CLONE (RIGHT) WITH TRACING PAPER ACTIVATED.

When you want to view your brushwork without the ghosted background image, simply deselect the tracing paper option. It's that simple. Figure 8.7 shows the original image and the cloned image with Tracing Paper turned off.

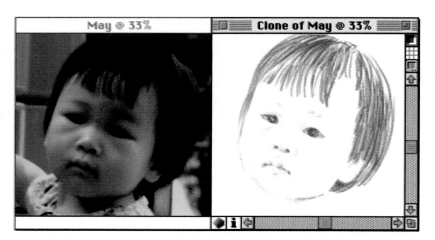

FIGURE 8.7 ORIGINAL (LEFT) AND CLONE (RIGHT) WITH TRACING PAPER OFF.

You can also trace part of an image by making a selection as Figure 8.8 shows.

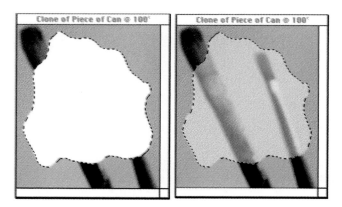

FIGURE 8.8 SELECTING A TRACING AREA *IMAGE* (LEFT); TURNING ON TRACING PAPER *IMAGE* (RIGHT).

CLONING TRANSFORMATIONS

Ready for something really exciting Take the idea of point-to-point cloning and multiply it by two, three, or four points. This advanced technique allows you to perform transformations such as scaling, rotating, and other distortions while at the same time painting an effect with a cloning brush.

The Super Cloner brush has variants for all the multiple point cloning options. The **Super Cloning Brush** (Mac) or **Scloners.brs** (Windows) is in the New Brushes library folder, which is in the Painter 5 demo folder. Select **Load Library...** from the last item on the Brush Type pop-up menu, and follow through the prompts to locate the Super Cloner brush.

Another way to access the multiple-point cloning options is to use the Cloner brush type or change any brush type's method to cloning. This will activate the Cloning palette, which you'll find under the Brush palette's Control menu. Clicking **Clone Color** on the Color palette will also enable the Cloning palette.

CLONE TYPES

Before we explore how to use the Clone Types feature, let's go over your options, as shown in the following list:

- ❑ *Normal* (0 points) Duplicates pixel information exactly, creating a clone from an original.
- ❑ *Offset* (1 point) Click and hold down the **Control** (Mac) or **Shift** (Windows) key to determine the point of origin, and then paint somewhere else.
- ❑ *Rotate and Scale* (2 points) Changes the size and angle of cloned imagery.
- ❑ *Scale* (2 points) Changes the size of cloned imagery.
- ❑ *Rotate* (2 points) Changes the angle of cloned imagery.
- ❑ *Rotate and Mirror* (2 points) Flips and changes the angle of cloned imagery.
- ❑ *Rotate, Scale, and Shear* (3 points) Skews the imagery as well as changes its size and angle.
- ❑ *Bilinear* (4 points) Plots four points that are the base for a fill.
- ❑ *Perspective* (4 points) The perspective of the original image is altered in the cloned image.

LINKING POINTS

Multiple cloning can be effected in the same document as the original or your link can be set in another document. You go about setting up these reference points with a combination of key commands and clicking and dragging. The key commands for setting points in the original (the source) are **Control** (Mac) or **Shift** (Windows). The key commands for setting points in the clone (destination) are **Control-Shift** (Mac) or **Ctrl+Shift** (Windows). For each, depending upon the option you are choosing, you click the correct number of points as you hold down the keys. To adjust the points, you need to continue to hold

down the keys as you drag. Figure 8.9 shows an example of setting points for Rotate and Scale in the source image.

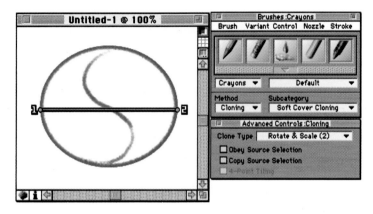

FIGURE 8.9 SETTING POINTS IN THE SOURCE IMAGE FOR THE ROTATE AND SCALE OPTION.

After these points are set, set the points for the clone. Figure 8.10 shows the painted clone with an overprint of the points set to change size and angle.

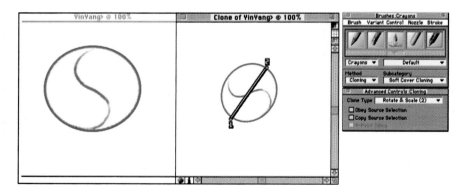

FIGURE 8.10 THE PAINTED CLONE WITH THE POINTS FOR ROTATE AND SCALE.

CLONING SELECTIONS

You'll probably want to isolate areas, through selections, for cloning. Click **Obey Source Selection** on the Cloning palette, and you're home free. The reference points won't pick up information that is not selected. To retain pixel-

depth information (as when cloning a photograph or other highly detailed image), click the **Copy Source Selection** option on the Cloning palette. You can also select both of these options at the same time.

WARPED FILLS

The Bilinear clone type is mainly used as a warped fill, but you may uncover some other applications for it in the course of your experimentation.

Open the source image, make a clone, and delete its contents. With the Bilinear clone type selected, either in the Cloning palette or from the Super Cloners variant pop-up menu, set the four points on the original by clicking and holding the **Control** (Mac) or **Shift** (Windows) keys. Make the clone document active and click points while holding down the **Control-Shift** (Mac) or **Ctrl-Shift** (Windows) keys. Under the Effects menu, select **Fill**, and in the Fill dialog box, check the **Clone Source** option. Click **OK**, and your clone document fills with a warped, tiled clone of your source selection. Figure 8.11 shows the filled clone with an overlay of the reference points.

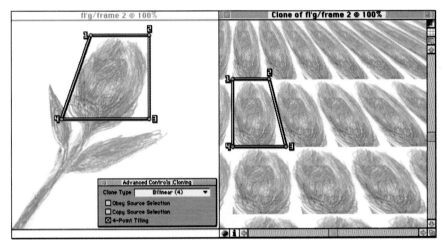

FIGURE 8.11 FILLING WITH THE BILINEAR CLONE TYPE.

You can also paint with any brush for a different effect, as Figure 8.12 shows.

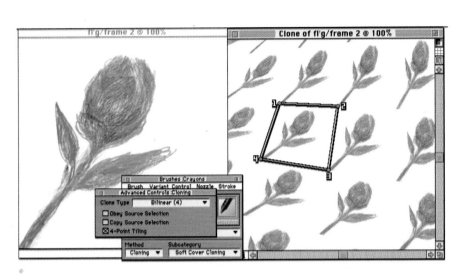

FIGURE 8.12 PAINTING A WARPED REPEAT.

PRACTICE EXERCISE

This exercise takes advantage of Painter's vast array of brushes by selecting the Cloning method when you choose any brush and its variant. The object of this exercise is to experience the flexibility of cloning by useing an existing image as a base from which to build a painting or illustration.

1. To begin, open the Tiger file from the Image Club folder on the CD. Select **Clone** from the File menu. Painter duplicates the tiger image. To get to Tracing Paper mode, choose **All** from the Select menu, and press **Delete** (Mac) or the **Backspace** key (Windows) to clear the canvas. Immediately select **Tracing Paper** from the Canvas menu to see the ghosted tiger image in the background.

2. Next, select any brush and begin to trace. Click on **Clone Color** in the Color palette to automatically pick up the color from the original image. Use the **Controls** palette to change your brush size and opacity as you draw. Build your painting using different brush types and variants.

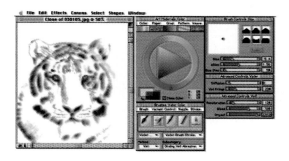

3. When you are through, deselect the Tracing Paper option. You may also toggle the Tracing Paper option on and off while you're painting to see how your image is progressing.

CHAPTER 9

MOSAICS AND TESSELLATIONS

Painter's Mosaics and Tessellations feature emulates the arts of mosaic painting and of stained glass imagery. Instead of dipping your digital brush into paint, you can load it up with tiles to create some sensational results. Then applying a 3-D effect gives it extra zing.

SOME BASIC RULES

Mosaics and Tessellations can be made from scratch or cloned from any kind of image.

Consider this feature as a standalone program embedded in Painter. All the action takes place in the Make Mosaic... and Make Tessellation... dialog boxes, found under Canvas on Painter's Main menu bar. While you are involved in creating a mosaic or tessellation piece, you can choose colors from the Color palette, use the Controls palette to select a different color, and take advantage of the help menu, but the other features of the program are inaccessible.

An excellent aspect of Mosaics and Tessellations is that both are resolution-independent. This means that you can create an elaborate painting or element and resize it up without any loss of quality.

Painter's brushes let you overlay colors, but Mosaic tiles work differently, as you'll soon see: once you lay down a tile, you cannot lay another tile over it. For this reason, when going for a classic mosaic look, draw the outlines first, and then fill in the rest, using the outlines as a guide for direction and evenness.

RENDERING TILES

When you have finished working in Mosaic mode, click **Done** and Painter renders your image onto the canvas. That sounds complicated, but it just means you're back to Painter's usual interface, and can implement all the features once again.

As mentioned before, you have the option of re-rendering a mosaic to change its resolution. Re-rendering an image erases any nonmosaic on the base canvas except for items that are deliberately above the canvas, such as floaters and shapes. For this reason, if you create mosaics to be part of a painting or element, it is strongly advised that you treat them separately by saving them in their own files and compositing them with other images until you've completed the painting. (You can either float the mosaic to composite it, or float other elements to composite with the mosaics. Refer to Chapter 6 for details on floaters and image-compositing options.)

SAVING A MOSAIC

The RIFF file format is the only format that supports Painter's Mosaics and Tessellations, keeping the image's tiles intact. Therefore, if you think you might want to do more work on your tiled images, always save the document as a RIFF file.

LAYING TILES

Painting with tiles follows the same basic principle of laying down ceramic tiles, which is that no tile can overlay another. If you try to do this, Painter will change the shape of the tile to fit the dimensions of the available space, which can make for some pretty interesting results (if you don't mind the spontaneity factor).

Unlike using their real-world counterparts, you have a number of options for modifying tiles once they're laid down. You can selectively erase them, and you can change or shift their colors in the blink of an eye. If, after working a while, you don't like the way the drawing is going along, you can remove all the tiles in the file with one move by selecting **Reset Mosaic**. Figure 9.1 shows you how.

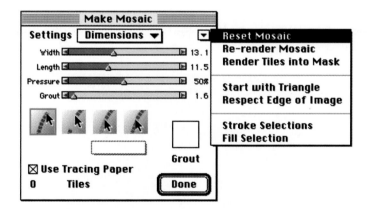

FIGURE 9.1 SELECTING RESET MOSAIC TO ERASE ALL THE TILES.

MOSAIC TOOLS

All these preliminaries probably have you ready to get started creating your own mosaics and tessellations, so let's review all the options in the Make Mosaic... dialog box, shown in Figure 9.2.

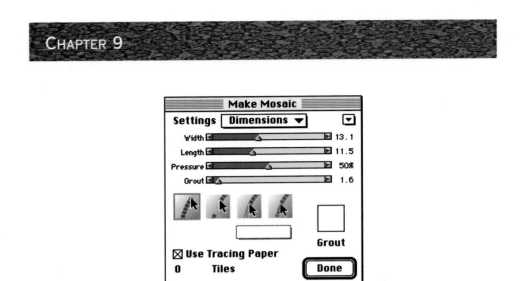

FIGURE 9.2 THE MAKE MOSAIC DIALOG BOX.

SETTINGS

Two options on the Settings pop-up menu control the nature of your tiles. These options are Dimensions and Randomness.

The Dimensions sliders control the basic shape of the tiles and the grout between them.

❑ **Width** determines the width of the tiles. Figure 9.3 shows different width settings.

FIGURE 9.3 TILE WIDTHS.

❑ **Length** sets the length of the tiles. Figure 9.4 shows different length settings.

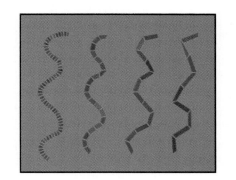

FIGURE 9.4 TILE LENGTHS.

❑ **Pressure** allows you to vary tile width based on stylus pressure. Set this option to 0 if you don't want stylus pressure to affect the width of your tiles. With this option, the greater the pressure on your stylus means the greater the width of your tile. Figure 9.5 shows different pressure settings.

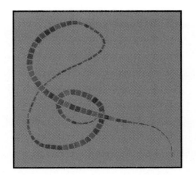

FIGURE 9.5 VARYING TILE WIDTH USING STYLUS PRESSURE.

❑ **Grout** determines the amount of space left between tiles. Figure 9.6 shows different grout settings.

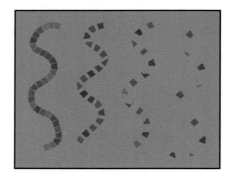

FIGURE 9.6 CHANGING GROUT SIZE.

The Randomness sliders control the uniformity (or lack thereof) among tiles. Set a slider to 0 if you want completely uniform tiles.

❑ **Width** A higher setting results in greater variability in tile width, as shown in Figure 9.7.

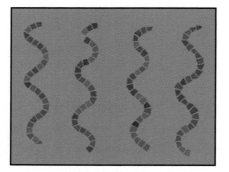

FIGURE 9.7 VARIABLE TILE WIDTH.

❑ **Length** A higher setting results in greater variability in tile length, as shown in Figure 9.8.
❑ **Cut** A higher setting changes the angle of the corners of each tile, as shown in Figure 9.9.
❑ **Grout** A higher setting varies the space between tiles, as shown in Figure 9.10.

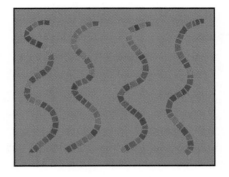

FIGURE 9.8 VARIABLE TILE LENGTH.

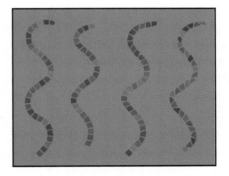

FIGURE 9.9 VARIABLE TILE CUT.

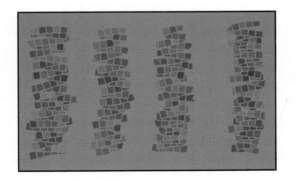

FIGURE 9.10 VARIABLE GROUT SIZE.

TILE TOOLS

There are four tile tools:

❏ **Apply Tiles** lets you draw with tiles. Simply click and drag the tool across the canvas, as with any brush.

❏ **Remove Tiles** is the Mosaic mode equivalent of an eraser. If you want to back up a bit and re-lay some tiles, choose this option, and selectively draw to erase tiles.

❏ **Change Tile Color** enables a pop-up menu below the tool. This menu lets you select a number of ways to change the color of a tile. Clicking with this tool changes the color of a tile to the current color selected on the Color palette.

❏ **Color** changes the color of a tile to the current color selected on the Color palette. Moving the H, S, and V (hue, saturation, value) sliders on the Color palette varies the color as you lay the tiles down.

❏ **Darken** adds a hint of black to a tile.

❏ **Lighten** adds a small amount of white to a tile.

❏ **Tint** adds 10 percent of the current color to a tile.

❏ **Vary** lets you use the variability settings on the Color palette to vary the color of your tiles. Traditionally, mosaics used tiles with many different colors, so you'll get more realistic results if you use this option.

Figure 9.11 shows these options. You can first select tiles with the Select Tiles tool before you apply color to them, or simply drag across the tiles you want to modify.

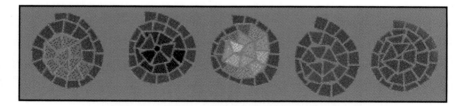

FIGURE 9.11 FROM LEFT TO RIGHT: ADDING, DARKENING, LIGHTENING, TINTING, AND VARYING COLOR.

❏ **Select Tiles** lets you choose specific tiles to work with. Click and drag across the tiles you want to select. Selected tiles are highlighted with red borders. Hold down the **Option** (Mac) or **Control** (Windows) key and click on a tile to select all tiles with the same color.

GROUT

Anything that is not a tile is grout. Click on the Grout square to change the color of the spaces between your tiles. This automatically re-renders your mosaic.

TRACING PAPER

You can use tracing paper to create a mosaic image. Open the image you would like to trace, and select **Clone** from the File menu. Working with the cloned image, check **Use Tracing Paper** in the Make Mosaic dialog box and begin tracing.

THE POP-UP MENU

There are a few Mosaic options left, and they are found on the little pop-up menu shown in Figure 9.12.

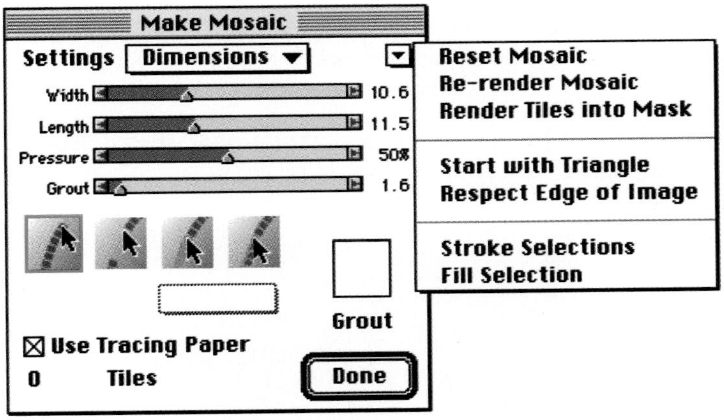

FIGURE 9.12 THE MAKE MOSAIC POP-UP MENU.

❑ **Reset Mosaic** removes all of the tiles from a mosaic. All that's left is the grout.
❑ **Re-render Mosaic** allows you to change the resolution of your file. For example, create a mosaic in 72 dpi (this makes life much easier), resize it to 300 dpi when you are through with it (it will be blurry until you re-render it), and then select **Re-render Mosaic** to replace the blurry tiles with crisp, new ones. It's cool, fast, and easy.

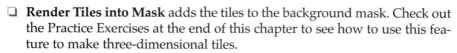
❏ **Render Tiles into Mask** adds the tiles to the background mask. Check out the Practice Exercises at the end of this chapter to see how to use this feature to make three-dimensional tiles.

❏ **Start with Triangle** makes the first tile in each stroke a triangle. This option is useful when working with angles spaces, as shown in Figure 9.13.

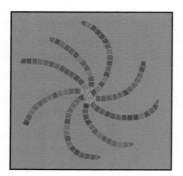

FIGURE 9.13 USING THE START WITH TRIANGLE FEATURE TO MAKE WEDGES AUTOMATICAL-LY. WE HAVE MADE THE FIRST TILE OF EACH STROKE RED TO MAKE IT EASIER TO SEE THE RESULT OF THIS FEATURE.

❏ **Respect Edge of Image** adds a grout rule around the edge of an image, as shown in Figure 9.14.

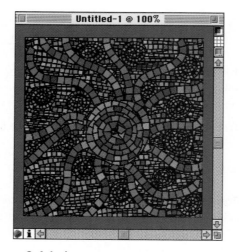

FIGURE 9.14 ADDING GROUT AROUND AN IMAGE.

❏ **Stroke Selections** lets you apply tiles to the outline of a selection, as shown in Figure 9.15.

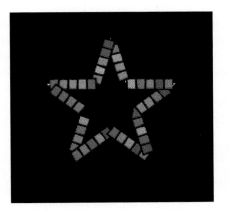

FIGURE 9.15 STROKING A SELECTION.

❏ **Fill Selection** applies tiles to the inside of a selection, as shown in Figure 9.16.

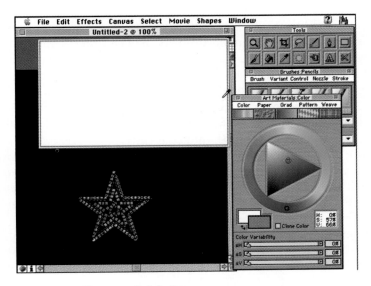

FIGURE 9.16 FILLING A SELECTION.

MAKING A TESSELLATION

A tessellation is simply a mosaic made of polygon-shaped tiles (as opposed to the rectangular shapes of mosaic tiles). The polygons are made up of points, and the more points you add, the more tiles appear in your image.

Tessellations are created differently than are mosaics, though most of the features in the Make Mosaic dialog box are available to modify a tessellation once it is made.

Select **Make Tessellation...** from the Canvas menu to open the Tessellation dialog box shown in Figure 9.17.

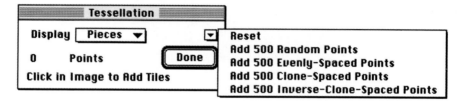

FIGURE 9.17 THE TESSELLATION DIALOG BOX.

Use the pop-up menu to select the type of points for your tiles: Triangles, Cracks, or Pieces. Next, select an option from the pop-up menu to add points to your tiles and to choose how they are placed (evenly or randomly). Unless your computer is very souped-up, it is likely to take a moment for it to process this command. You can keep returning to this pop-up menu, adding points to your tessellation, but remember that as the point number increases so does required processing power, so don't add more points than your computer or your patience is capable of. When you have finished making specifications for your tessellation, click **Done**. Painter converts your tessellation into mosaic tiles and renders the tile onto your canvas.

Once you create a tessellation you can go back into the Make Mosaic dialog box and fine-tune your image. Please note, however, that in order to activate Apply Tiles, you first have to use Remove Tiles or Reset Mosaic. You can also use the commands Reset Mosaic, Re-Render Mosaic, and Render Tiles into Mask. If you haven't selected a grout color, you can do that, too.

To generate a tessellation based on a clone, open a document, clone it, then open the Make Tessellation dialog box. Use the clone-related commands on the pop-up menu. After you've clicked **Done**, you can return to the Make Mosaic dialog box, select **Render Tiles into Mask**, click **Done**, and apply a **3-D Surface** texture for some really great results.

PRACTICE EXERCISE

This exercise uses most of the features in the Make Mosaic... dialog box. The object of this exercise is to see how easy it is to transform an image into a stylized mosaic painting. You can use the underlying image as a base, and embellish it with mosaic tiles.

1. To start, open the Fish.high.tif file from the Image Club folder on the CD. Select **Clone** from the File menu and Painter reproduces the fish image. Choose **All** from the Select menu, then press **Delete**

(Mac) or the **Backspace** key (Windows). Select **Make Mosaic** from the Canvas menu and click **Use Tracing Paper**. Make sure Clone Color is selected on the Color palette or else your tiles will use the currently selected color.

2. Next, outline the fish, then fill in the details. If you need to rework an area, remember that you can remove tiles and replace them. Periodically turn off the Use Tracing Paper option to check your work.

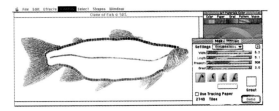

3. Add tiles to the background. Move the H, S, and V sliders on the Color palette to vary the colors of the tiles, or use the **Tint** or **Vary** option, under the Color Tiles icon, to change colors. Click **Done**, and your tiles are rendered onto the Painter canvas.

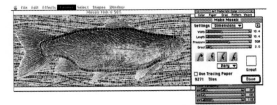

CHAPTER 10

RECORDING
YOUR SCRIPTS

Painter can literally record your brush strokes and special effects to be saved for playback at a later time. Recording a script is the same action as recording a tape or video: Start recording and stop when you're through; then, play it back when needed. It's really that simple.

If you've ever created a drawing at 72 pixels per inch and then resized it to 300 pixels per inch, you may have been disappointed in the blurry, imprecise results. You can get around this problem if you record the lower-resolution session and then play back your brush strokes at the higher resolution. Painter automatically re-creates your image at the higher resolution as it re-scales all the brushes, paper textures, masks, and effects you've used.

If you find you are using the same brush stroke on an image over and over again, you can simply record the stroke or strokes and play back over the script. Once the stroke is recorded, you can change the brush, its attributes, and its color as it plays.

This feature is also useful when you are teaching or demonstrating. Instead of re-creating your examples, simply record them once, the first time—then play them back ad infinitum.

Recording script options are available on the Objects: Scripts palette, shown in Figure 10.1. The palette controls work just like the controls on a VCR: Stop, Play, Record, Pause, and Advance (from left to right).

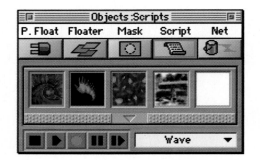

FIGURE 10.1 THE OBJECTS: SCRIPTS PALETTE.

RECORDING AND PLAYING BACK INDIVIDUAL BRUSH STROKES

This feature is great if you have multiple strokes to apply, or just want to generate an interesting texture. This is one of those efficiency tasks computers are meant for, so why not let Painter do the work for you?

To record a brush stroke, you must first have a file open. On the Brushes palette, click on **Stroke**, and select **Record Stroke** from its menu.

STROKE PLAYBACK

To play back the stroke, select **Playback Stroke** from the Stroke menu; then click in your image wherever you want to place the stroke. The stroke is replayed each time you click, as shown in Figure 10.2.

FIGURE 10.2 PLAYING BACK A RECORDED BRUSH STROKE.

When you are through playing back your stroke, stop the playback feature by deselecting **Playback** from the Stroke menu (that is, uncheck it).

Once your brush stroke is recorded, you can vary it by changing brushes and colors. For example, if you record a stroke using the Artist Pastel Chalk variant in blue and then change your selected variant to the Feather Tip Airbrush variant using green, your recorded stroke changes accordingly. Figure 10.3 shows the recorded stroke played back using different brush variants and colors.

FIGURE 10.3 PLAYING BACK THE STROKE USING DIFFERENT VARIANTS AND COLORS.

You can also choose **Auto Playback** from the Stroke menu. This selection starts to fill in your image with your recorded stroke in a random pattern, using the latest brush and color you have chosen. When the stroke has filled in your image to your satisfaction, simply click once in the image, and the playback stops.

PLAYBACK WITHIN MASKS AND SELECTIONS

You can confine your stroke playback to a selection, using either Playback Stroke or Auto Playback. To see how Auto Playback works with a selection, select the area with the lasso tool or rectangular selection tool, and choose **Auto Playback** from the Stroke menu. When the area fills up with the stroke, as in Figures 10.4 and 10.5, click once, and the playback will stop. This happens quickly, so be ready to act fast!

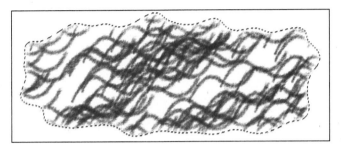

FIGURE 10.4 FILLING A LASSO SELECTION USING AUTO PLAYBACK.

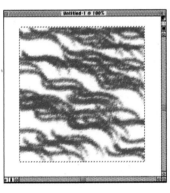

FIGURE 10.5 FILLING A RECTANGULAR SELECTION USING AUTO PLAYBACK.

RECORDING A WORK SESSION

There are quite a few reasons to record an entire work session. Some reasons are:

❏ To play back at a higher resolution

- ❏ To have a record for teaching or demonstrating
- ❏ To reuse techniques in other projects
- ❏ To have a record of how you created an effect

The first two of these reasons were covered in the opening of this chapter; let's take a moment to expand a little on the last two reasons. If you develop a particular technique that you want to apply on other images, by recording it, you will preserve the key steps needed to replicate that look. Also, instead of trying to reconstruct how you arrived at a particular solution, by recording as you go, your method is preserved intact.

SCRIPT OPTIONS

Select **Script Options...** from the Script menu (on the Object palette). The Script Options dialog box, shown in Figure 10.6, is displayed.

FIGURE 10.6 THE SCRIPT OPTIONS DIALOG BOX.

If you check Record Initial State, the session is recorded intact, including the brush variants, colors, and paper textures used during the session. The currently selected brush variant, color, and paper texture do not affect the playback.

If you uncheck Record Initial State, the playback is dependent on the currently selected brush variant, color, and paper texture.

If you would like your session to be recorded as a movie, select the **Save Frames on Playback** option and specify how often (in nths of a second) you want to save frames.

RECORDING

Click the red **Record** button on the Objects: Scripts palette and begin making your brush strokes. Change variants, colors, and textures and add all of the

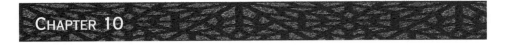
special effects you want—Painter keeps track of them. When you are through with your session, click the **Stop** button.

Enter a session title in the Name the Script dialog box that is displayed and click **OK**. Your session is now added to the current library. There is no limit to the number of sessions you can record.

SCRIPT PLAYBACK

When you're ready to play back your session, open the icon drawer on the Objects: Scripts palette, as in Figure 10.7. You'll see icons for the finished product from each session you have in the open library.

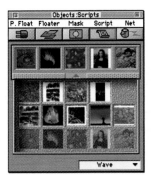

FIGURE 10.7 THE LIBRARY DRAWER ON THE OBJECTS: SCRIPTS PALETTE.

Select the Script icon to play back, close the drawer, and then click the **Play** button. Painter replays your work session.

If you want to cancel a script while it is in progress, press **Command-.** (period) on the Mac, or **Ctrl-.** in Windows.

PLAYBACK AT A NEW RESOLUTION

You may record at one resolution and then play back at another, but you must follow a specific set of steps for playback to work properly.

RECORDING

Open a new image file and choose **All** from the Select menu. Click the **Record** button; then choose **None** from the Select menu, or draw inside the selected area. Begin your work and save your session as usual.

PLAYBACK

Open a new image file with a different resolution but the same dimensions. Choose **All** from the Select menu; then click on the **Play** button. Your session is replayed in the selected area.

RECORDING A SCRIPT AS A MOVIE

You can turn a recorded script into a movie and export it as a QuickTime movie (Mac) or AVI video (Windows).

Before you record your script, be sure that **Save Frames on Playback** is checked in the Record Initial dialog box and specify how often you would like frames saved. The more often you save frames, the smoother your movie will be. However, because more frames result in more disk space used, you'll want to evaluate the trade-off.

Record a script as usual, select its icon from the library drawer, and click the **Play** button to replay it. You'll see a dialog box asking you to name the frame stack for the movie. Enter a name and location and click on **Save**.

In the New Frame Stack dialog box, enter the storage type and the number of onion-skin layers you want and click **OK**. Your session is now saved as a frame stack. To save the stack as a QuickTime or AVI movie, use the **Save As...** function under the File menu to change the file name and file type.

CREATING LIBRARIES OF SCRIPTS

As with many of Painter's features, you can create libraries of recorded scripts, organized in any way that suits your working habits.

NEW LIBRARIES

Painter automatically saves scripts you create into the current library. To change libraries or create a new one before you begin a new script, select **Load Library** from the pop-up menu list on the Objects: Scripts palette. Locate the library you want or enter a name in the dialog box. You can also use the **Scripts Mover...** option, under the Scripts menu, to create a new library and to move scripts between libraries for more efficient management of your files. Refer to Chapter 5 for a review of how libraries and movers work.

OPENING A LIBRARY

To open an existing library, click the **Library** button on the Scripts icon drawer. From the File Open dialog box, select the library you want to open. Click **OK**. You may now select and play back any session saved in that library.

PRACTICE EXERCISE

This exercise covers the basic features you'll use to record a work session. The object of this exercise is to demonstrate how easy and practical recording a script can be. We're going to paint a copy of an existing image so that your artistic concerns about composition are minimized, and you can instead concentrate on tackling this technological feat!

1. To begin, open the "Mountain Mist" file from the Image Club folder on the CD-ROM. We're going to create a new file that is roughly the same size: 7.5 inches by 5 inches, at 72 pixels per inch. We're going to record this session with the canvas at this resolu-

   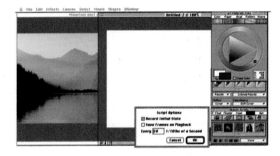

   tion, then re-create it at a higher resolution. Select **Script Options** from the Script menu, and make sure that the **Record Initial State** option is checked. Choose **All** from the Select menu, then click on the **Record** button on the Objects: Scripts palette.

2. Begin painting the mountain scene, using Mountain Mist as reference. Try out a variety of colors, brushes, textures, and effects. Really take your time. Remember that you are not creating a huge file, because Painter records the information as text, not as pixels. When you are

   through with your painting, click the **Stop** button (the black square), name the file, and click **OK**. This second picture shows the finished painting.

3. Create a new document with the same dimensions, but at a higher resolution of 150 pixels per inch. Choose **All** from the Select menu. Select the name for the mountain session you just created, click the **Play** button (the black triangle), and watch it play back at a

higher resolution. This third picture shows a playback at roughly two-thirds through the session. Note that the canvas is larger, due to the increased resolution.

CHAPTER 11

MOVIES AND ANIMATION

You can use any of Painter's tools and special effects to enhance any movie or animation or to create your own. Your work can be based on video, illustration, or both. For the most part, everything you learned earlier in this book can be applied to movies. A few simple rules and exceptions are covered in this chapter. Because Painter works with QuickTime (Mac) and AVI (Windows) and frame stacks to create animations, let's first go through their basics.

QUICKTIME AND AVI

QuickTime is a Mac file format that lets your computer support sound, video, and animation. It also lets you export to Windows systems. Painter takes QuickTime data and turns it into a Painter frame stack. Painter frame stacks can be exported into QuickTime files for use with Mac or Windows video-editing software.

AVI is a Windows file format for saving sound, video, and animation files, and is the more popular format among Windows users. As with QuickTime, AVI has a number of compression formats to choose from.

FRAME STACKS

A frame stack is a series of images in Painter that make up a movie or animation.

Images in a frame stack must be numbered sequentially, with the number preceded by a period (.). Each numbered file must use the same number of digits. If you have fewer than ten numbered files, you can use the format **Movie.1** through **Movie.9**. However, if you have more than ten numbered files—21, for example—you must use the format **Movie.01** through **Movie.21**.

OPENING MOVIE FILES

Use the same procedure to open a Painter movie or QuickTime or AVI file as you would any other Painter file. A dialog box will open, asking for a new file name, because it is creating a frame stack. Name it and be sure to place it on a drive that has plenty of free space, then click **OK**.

You'll see a dialog box asking how many layers of onion skin you would like in your file. This refers to the onion-skin paper traditionally used by animators. This paper allows animators to see a number of frames at once through layers of transparent paper, so that users can align with and view previous frames as they create new ones. Painter allows the use of two to five layers of onion skin. Select the number of layers, as in Figure 11.1, and click **OK**.

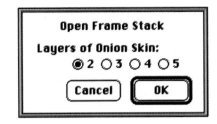

FIGURE 11.1 SELECTING THE NUMBER OF ONION-SKIN LAYERS.

Painter automatically saves changes made to a frame once you move to another frame. It is a good idea to always duplicate your file or save your file to another name before making any changes, but be forewarned that file sizes can be hefty.

OPENING NUMBERED FILES

If you are opening numbered files, click on the **Open Numbered Files** check box at the bottom of the Open dialog box, shown in Figure 11.2. You are prompted to select the first file in the sequence; do that and then click **Open**. Next, you'll be asked to select the last file in the sequence. Select it, click **Open**, and select the number of onion-skin layers, as before.

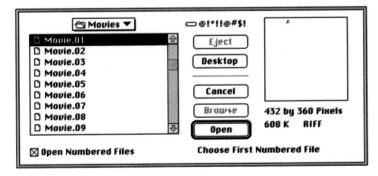

FIGURE 11.2 OPENING NUMBERED FILES.

CREATING A NEW MOVIE

Let's move through the basic sequence you'll follow to create an animation to show how this feature works.

To start a new movie file, go to **File: New**. At the bottom of the dialog box, under Picture Type, select **Movie**, and type in the number of frames you want your movie to be. In this case, enter the number **4**.

Next, under Canvas Size, type in **5 inches** for the width and for the height, and **72.0** for the resolution. Figure 11.3 shows how your New Picture dialog box will appear.

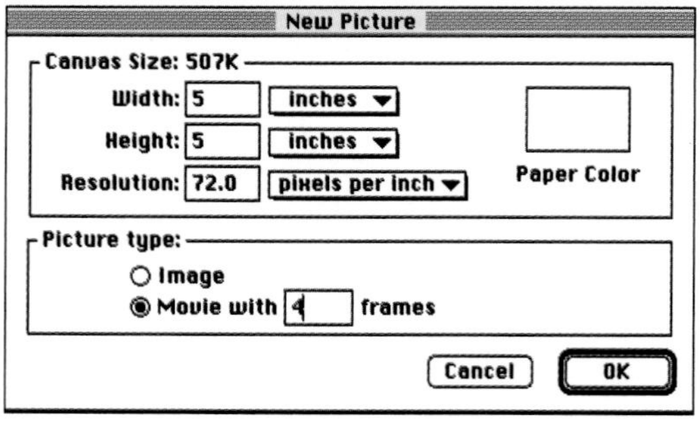

FIGURE 11.3 CREATING A NEW MOVIE FILE.

When you click **OK**, another dialog box appears. This dialog box functions as a Save As… dialog box, prompting you to name the movie and to select or create a new folder for it. Next, when you click **OK**, the New Frame Stack dialog box appears. Here you enter the number of onion-skin layers and select file storage, as shown in Figure 11.4.

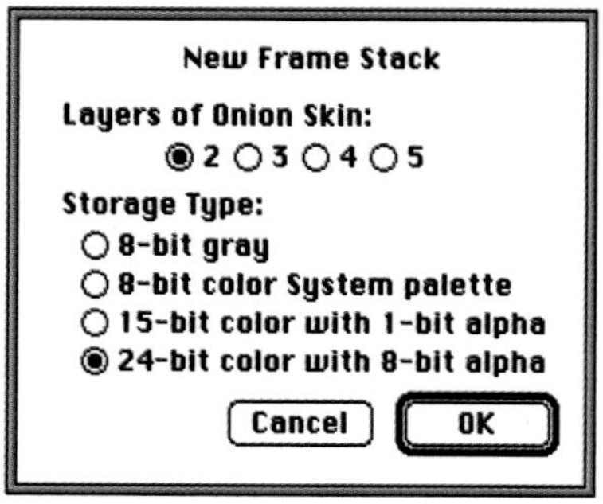

FIGURE 11.4 THE NEW FRAME STACK DIALOG BOX.

Images in a frame stack must be of equal size and resolution. They can be saved in the following ways:

- ❏ 256-level gray (8-bit gray)
- ❏ 256 color palette (8-bit color)
- ❏ 32,768 colors plus a mask layer (15-bit color and a 1-bit mask)
- ❏ 16.7 million colors plus an antialiased mask layer (24-bit color and an 8-bit mask)

For now, accept the default, and you will see a blank new image and the Frame Stacks palette. Let's go over its various functions before starting to draw.

THE FRAME STACKS PALETTE

The Frame Stacks palette is displayed any time you open an existing movie file or create a new one. This palette, shown in Figure 11.5, not only displays a thumbnail of each movie frame and the number of frames in the current movie, it also indicates the current frame with a red arrow and has button controls that work much like the controls on your VCR.

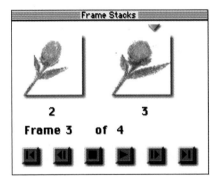

FIGURE 11.5 THE FRAME STACKS PALETTE.

 Go to the first frame. You may also use the **Home** key.

 Go forward, one frame at a time. You may also use the **Page Up** key.

 Stop playing. You may also use **Command-.** (period) (Mac) or **Control-+** (Windows).

 Play the entire movie.

Go backward one frame at a time. You may also use the **Page Down** key.

Go to the last frame. You may also use the **End** key.

Draw a flower bud and stem in the image, using any brushes and tools to do this. This will be your first frame. Plan your drawing so that the budding flower will open to full bloom. When you are through, go to **Select: All** and then go to **Edit: Copy**. You are going to drop this first frame into the second frame and draw or paint the progressive changes there. Figure 11.6 shows an example of the first frame.

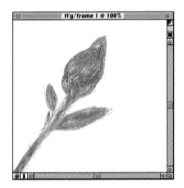

FIGURE 11.6 THE FIRST FRAME OF A BUDDING FLOWER ANIMATION.

Advance to the second frame, then select **Paste: Normal** from the Edit menu. The copied first frame will come into the second as a floater, which we'll drop (see Chapter 6 for more information on floaters), by opening the **Objects: Floater** palette and clicking on the **Drop** option at the bottom of the palette window. Switch back to the Brush tool and begin to paint in the second frame. Continue doing this until you have four different frames, depicting four different stages of the flower. When you are through, click on the **Play** button in the Frame Stacks palette to see your frames linked into an animation. Figure 11.7 shows an example of the progressive frames: frames 2, 3, and 4.

In addition to the controls on the Frame Stacks palette, you may use the **Page Up** and **Page Down** keys to move from frame to frame. Also, you may use the first four options on the Movie menu to add frames, delete frames, erase contents of a frame (or range of frames), and go to a specific frame.

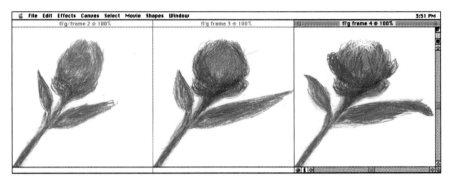

FIGURE 11.7 FRAMES 2, 3, AND 4 OF THE BLOOMING FLOWER.

To see this simple animation you have just completed, open the *Flowering* file from the *Animation Sample* folder on the CD-ROM.

APPLYING YOUR TOOLS TO MOVIES

You can apply any of Painter's standard tools to a movie. You can apply brushes, textures, masks, and special effects, either frame by frame or to the entire movie. To use a tool on a particular frame, simply go to that frame and use it as you normally would.

To apply a special effect, texture, or brush stroke to an entire movie, begin recording a session, apply your effect, and then stop recording the session. Be sure the movie is open; then select **Apply Script to Movie...** from the Movie menu. Select the session you want to apply and click **Playback**. Your special effect, texture, or brush stroke is applied to the entire movie.

You can also use Painter's cloning tools with individual frames in a movie. Just remember that your frame dimension and resolution must be the same for the source and clone images.

You can use the cloning tools to create Tracing Paper, as well as any of the cloning brushes. You may also use the masking tools to protect portions of an image and replace the unprotected part with a cloned image.

CHAPTER 12

NET PAINTER

Net Painter is the ultimate in performance art, collaborative art, teaching art. This is a very attention-worthy feature. This tool—the first of its kind—provides real-time collaboration and document sharing over a network or the Internet. Net Painter is an ideal way to:

❏ develop work between artists and clients
❏ teach numerous students at once
❏ collaborate with other artists across the globe
❏ share and work on documents with colleagues
❏ watch and learn from a famous artist's work

JUST A LITTLE TECHNICAL STUFF

Net Painter can be used on any TCP/IP network. If you can use Netscape or another browser to surf the World Wide Web (WWW), your computer uses TCP/IP. If you are not sure whether your computer is TCP/IP-capable, contact your modem manufacturer. Fractal Design Corporation technical support can help you paint using Net Painter, but you will need to contact your network administrator or hardware supplier if you have any networking questions.

The Net Painter feature works on Power Mac, and Window 95, or Windows NT systems.

NETWORKING BY MODEM

Technically, you can use Net Painter with a 14.4 Kbps modem, but for the most reasonable performance you should use a 28.8 Kbps (V.34) or 56 Kbps modem.

FILE TRANSFER

If you want to transfer any files or libraries, you will definitely want to invest in a 28.8 Kbps modem. File transfer is also slow across a network, so it is advisable to simply download files manually, especially if they're large.

Any non-default files—such as custom textures, brush variants, nozzles, floaters, paths, or any other libraries—must be transferred to the other users before starting your session. All the Net Painter options are found on the Objects Palette, either under the Net icon or Net menu, shown in Figure 12.1. To transfer a file to other collaborators, select **Send File on Net...** from the Net menu, choose the files you want to send, and click **Open**. Received files are sent to the Painter network folder.

Please note that with the upgrade of Painter, there is a slight incompatibility between Painter 4 and Painter 5, so it's best to work with the defaults common to both programs.

FIGURE 12.1 THE OBJECTS PALETTE WITH THE NETWORK ICON AND MENU.

WORKING WITH NET PAINTER

Before you begin working with Net Painter, you'll first need to fill in some setup information. Select **Setup** from the Network menu, and you'll see the dialog box shown in Figure 12.2.

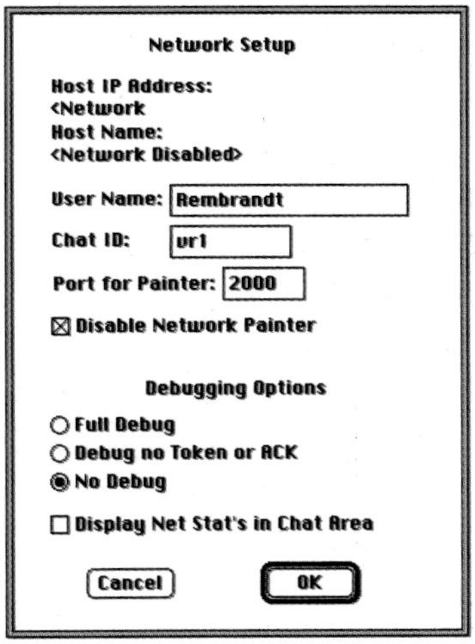

FIGURE 12.2 THE NETWORK SETUP DIALOG BOX.

Net Painter automatically enters your computer's Host IP address and computer domain name, if one is available. Enter your name in the User Name field. This is the name that is displayed beside the Traffic Light icon. You may also enter a Chat ID, which is like the screen name you use for an on-line service. Your chat ID can be up to four letters, numbers, or a combination of both.

Prior to signing on, you'll need to contact your collaborators to choose a port number. Everyone signing on to the same session must have the same port number, which can be any number between 1024 and 65535. Select **Disable Network Painter** to prevent anyone from signing onto your work session.

199

SIGNING ONTO A WORK SESSION

Everyone who wants to join a work session must be signed on before anyone begins working. Once a group member begins working, the session is closed and nobody else can join. So don't open a file or pick up a brush until the group is complete, because you're effectively locking the door.

To sign on, select **Connect** from the Network menu. Use the Network Connect dialog box to identify the machine you are connecting to. Your connection is defined by an IP address or domain name.

When the connection is made, the names of those connected are displayed in the top of the Network palette. If there are more than two users, any additional user can connect to any user who is currently signed onto a work session. Once a group member starts painting, the work session is locked and no one else can sign on.

PAINTING ON THE NET

Once everyone is signed on, someone can begin painting. Only one user can paint at a time. It's a bit irresistible to jump in, but Net Painter insists that everyone takes turns. To paint, click on the **Green Light** icon on the Network palette. If another user is already painting, a Yellow Light icon will be displayed beside your name. If more than one user is waiting to paint, you will be queued in the order in which you clicked the Green Light icon. The queue order is shown on the Network palette. When the current artist is finished, the next in line will be given the green light to paint, and so on. Painters who are just watching will have a Red Light icon posted next to their names.

CHATTING

If you want to send a suggestion, comment on a painter's work, or ask if the current artist could let you try for a while, you can send a message in the Chat window, on the lower half of the Network palette.

To chat, click on the **Chat** line at the bottom of the Network palette and begin typing: your message will appear in black and others will be in color. Press the **Return** (Mac) or **Enter** (Windows) key on your keyboard to send your message to all the other users in your work session. To exit chat mode, press **Return** (Mac) or **Enter** (Windows) again, with no text in the chat line.

SIGNING OFF

To sign off from a Net Painter work session, select **Close Connection** from the Network menu.

CHAPTER 13

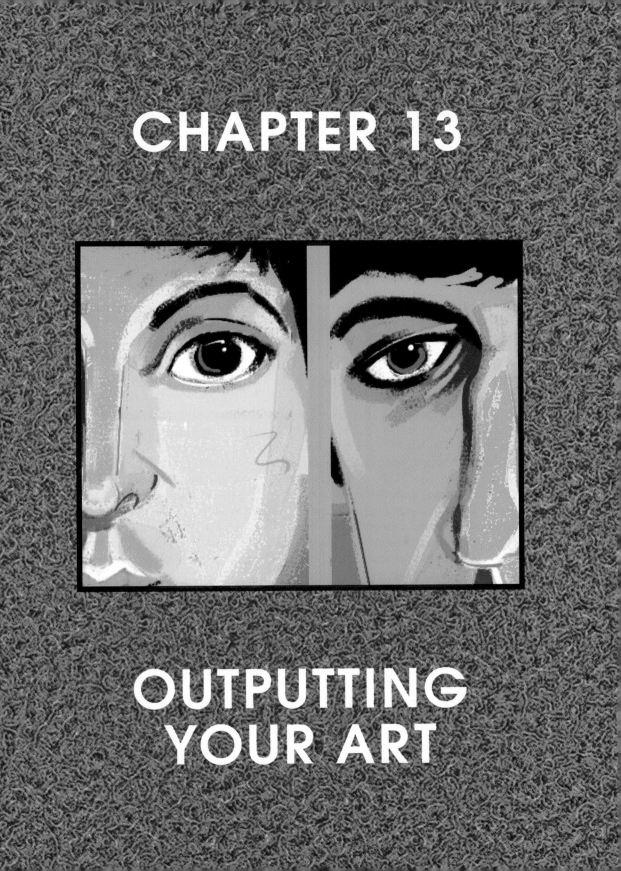

OUTPUTTING
YOUR ART

Well, you've arrived at the final stage of your creation. You've learned almost everything there is to know about creating digital art in Painter, and now it's time to send your work out into the world. The key question is how.

Choosing output that best shows off your art is equally important to the making of it. Fortunately, you have a variety of credible options for printers and, as the technology evolves, for materials to print on, such as watercolor paper, handmade paper, and canvas.

Painter supports any PostScript (Mac) or GDI (Windows) device. Many of the better options involve expensive equipment, but most metropolitan areas have service bureaus that provide access to these high-end machines at per-piece costs. If you don't live near a major city, you can still use these service bureaus via overnight shipping or high-speed modem.

We'll cover most of your options, but please check with your service bureau or in the manual for your printing device for specific instructions on file type and page setup requirements.

COLOR MONITOR CALIBRATION

A major issue with any digital art is monitor calibration: how accurate are the colors and value range you are viewing? There is often a huge gap between the monitor's display of color and the colors of the printed image (Chapter 3 opens with an explanation of why this is so), but we can narrow this gap greatly with just a little effort. If you have Photoshop, you can use the handy Gamma feature to match your monitor to the piece (proof) you hold in your hand or use any other color calibration device available. You can still achieve great results simply by proofing your work to a color printer and making the necessary adjustments within Painter. Under Effects on the Main Menu bar, select **Tonal Control** and scroll through the menu list to find the appropriate feature for your color shifts.

KODAK COLOR MANAGEMENT SYSTEM

Painter 5 incorporates the Kodak Color Management System to help you anticipate and correct potential color printing problems as your work progresses. It should be emphasized that this system will give only an approximation of the image's output because current technology has too many variables to promise an absolute match.

To see your image as it will print, activate the **Output Preview** option. The details of this feature are covered in Chapter 3. You can also select the **Show Gamut Warning** option to determine which colors your selected printer will not be able to print and to make the necessary changes to bring them into the printable range.

To print your image using the Kodak Color Management System (KCMS) you must have a Color Postscript printer. With Output Preview activated, KCMS will convert the document's colors to the range your printer can handle. This only prints the image in these colors and will not affect the colors in the original document.

You can also use the KCMS to create separation files for documents you intend to save as EPS, by activating the Output Preview option.

EXPORTING FILES

Painter files are created and saved using the RGB color model. To place illustrations in many page layout programs, you must use CMYK files. Although you can't convert your images to CMYK mode in Painter, you may open your Painter files in most image manipulation programs such as Photoshop or Digital Darkroom, and convert them there.

Decide which format is best suited to the program you'll be importing the Painter files and save the image in that format within the Save As dialog box. Select **Save As...** from the File menu, and you'll see the dialog box in Figure 13.1. Choose the file format you need for exporting your image from the Type (Mac) or Save As Type (Windows) pop-up menu, enter a file name in the Save Image As (Mac) or File Name (Windows) field, and click **OK**.

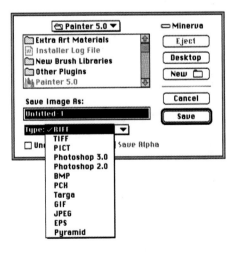

FIGURE 13.1 THE SAVE AS DIALOG BOX WITH EXPORTING OPTIONS ON THE POP-UP TYPE MENU.

Your exporting options are:

❏ *RIFF* (raster image file format). This is the default option. To save file space, always leave the Uncompressed option unchecked. RIFF files can only be used within Painter.

❏ *TIFF* (tagged image file format). This is a versatile graphics format that stores a map specifying the location and color associated with each pixel. TIFF is supported by IBM-compatible and NeXT systems.

❏ *PICT.* This collection of QuickDraw routines is needed to create an image. It is the main format used by the Macintosh clipboard.

❏ *Photoshop* (version 3 or 4). This is the native file format for Adobe Photoshop files. Photoshop files are always full 24-bit color.

❏ *BMP.* These bitmap files are the main format used by the Microsoft Windows (IBM-compatible computers) clipboard.

❏ *PCX* (picture exchange). This format is used by many scanners and paint-style programs.

❏ *Targa.* This file format is used by high-end, PC-based paint programs. Targa files have 24 bits per pixel.

❏ *GIF* (graphics interchange format). This is an 8-bit (or less) color format that is used for images placed in HTML documents to be displayed on the Internet.

❏ *JPEG* (joint photographers experts group). This file format compresses images and is used for storing images or for display in HTML documents on the Internet.

❏ *PYRAMID.* This format is used for large images, most often for recording scripts at a lower resolution to be played back at a higher resolution.

❏ *EPS* (encapsulated PostScript). Painter's EPS files conform to the EPS-DCS 5-file format used for desktop color separation. Please note that files saved in this format cannot be reopened by Painter. If you want to be able to reopen a file saved in this format, save it in another format (with another name) before saving it as an EPS file. Selecting EPS opens the EPS Options dialog box, shown in Figure 13.2.

❏ *Data Options*: Hex (ASCII) Picture Data. Select this option for programs that require it, such as PageMaker.

❏ *Preview Options*: Your selection depends upon whether you are printing in black or color and what you are using the images for. Selecting black and white preview will not affect the document's color information.

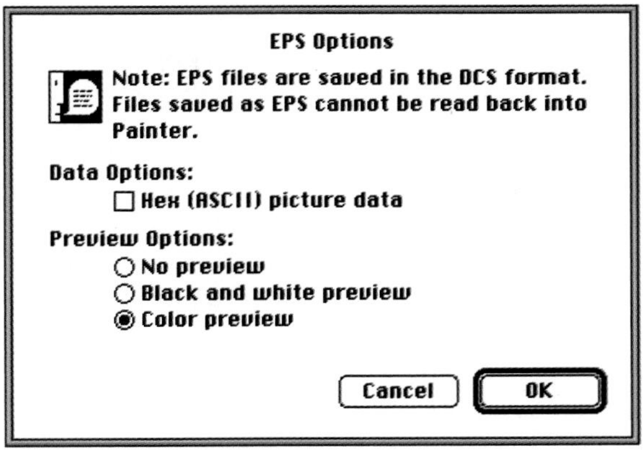

FIGURE 13.2 THE EPS OPTIONS DIALOG BOX.

PAGE SETUP OPTIONS

In addition to the file type, you may select from a number of page setup options for your images. To access these options, select Page Setup (Mac) or Print Setup (Windows) from the File menu. You'll see the dialog box shown in Figure 13.3.

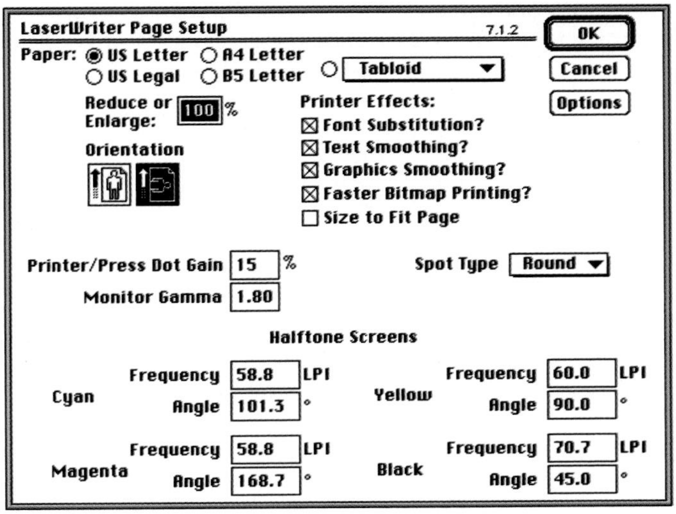

FIGURE 13.3 THE PAGE SETUP DIALOG BOX.

205

Paper Type, Printer Effects, and Orientation are relatively self-explanatory and are found as page setup options in most Mac programs. Printer/Press Dot Gain adjusts the size of halftone dots according to the requirements of your print shop.

Monitor Gamma refers to the brightness of your monitor. Unless you're using a monitor calibration device or you have a monitor that has other gamma requirements, you're pretty safe with the default setting. Spot Type determines the shape of your halftone dots.

Use the fields in the Halftone Screens area to change the settings for the grid of dots printed when using halftone screens (Frequency), or the angle at which the screens lay on your image (Angle). These settings may be adjusted for all four colors in the CMYK process.

PRINTING COMPOSITES

Because printing a composite in Painter might test your patience, an expedient method for printing composite images is to first clone the image, which will automatically drop all the shapes and floaters. Then print the clone, leaving your original intact.

IMAGE RESIZING AND RESOLUTION

Before outputting an image, you may want to change its dimensions (often called *resizing*) or resolution (often called *resampling*) to fit your output device. When outputting your work, the relationship between the image size and its resolution is very important.

Resolution refers to the numbers of pixels per inch (ppi) displayed on your monitor or the number of dots per inch (dpi) used in the printing process. Most monitors have a resolution of about 72 ppi; typical laser printers have a resolution of 300 dpi and can go as high as 600 dpi; imagesetters can have resolutions of 1200 dpi to more than 5000 dpi; and most color printers range from 260 dpi up past 300 dpi.

We'll say it again: Read the device user manual or contact your service bureau to determine the exact resolution requirements.

Select **Resize...** from the Canvas menu to access the Resize dialog box shown in Figure 13.4.

The lower half of the box provides current information about your document, including its dimensions and resolution. "Current Size" refers to the amount of RAM your image takes up, not to the amount of hard disk space it uses.

Resize

```
┌ Current Size: 157K ─────────────────────────┐
│       Width:    200      Pixels              │
│      Height:    200      Pixels              │
│  Resolution:    72.0     Pixels per Inch     │
└──────────────────────────────────────────────┘

┌ New Size: 157K ─────────────────────────────┐
│       Width:  [200   ]  [ pixels    ▼]       │
│      Height:  [200   ]  [ pixels    ▼]       │
│  Resolution:  [72.0  ]  [ pixels per inch ▼] │
└──────────────────────────────────────────────┘

  ☒ Constrain File Size

                          [ Cancel ]  [  OK  ]
```

FIGURE 13.4 THE RESIZE DIALOG BOX.

To resize your image, enter new values in the Width and Height fields. Change the resolution of an image using the Resolution field. Use the pop-up menus next to these fields to change the units of measurement for your image. Uncheck the **Constrain File Size** box when resizing, in order to give yourself greater flexibility over image size and resolution. When you have resized your image, click **OK** to accept your changes.

You can also find out your image size and resolution by clicking on the **i** in the lower left of your document window (next to the drawing mode icons). The pop-up box, shown in Figure 13.5, also shows how your image fits on the page size selected in the Page Setup (Mac) or Print Setup (Windows) dialog box.

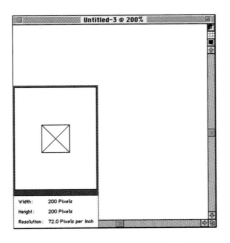

FIGURE 13.5 DISPLAYING IMAGE SIZE, RESOLUTION, AND PLACEMENT.

If you increase the size and resolution of your image, the program has to input new pixel information into the spaces you have, in effect, created. This can compromise the artwork's detail, by making it blurry. To preserve pixel information, the rule of thumb is to decrease *either* the size or the resolution when you must make these changes. For example, if you have created an image that is 10" by 10" at 150 ppi, and you want to print it out at 300 ppi, you can change its dimensions to 5" by 5" without losing anything. Painter does offer a way around this dilemma however: if you plan ahead and record your session(s), you can play back the scripts and re-create the image perfectly at a higher resolution. (Refer to Chapter 10 for the details.)

PRINTING

Once you have entered the relevant information in the Setup dialog box, and calculated the size and resolution of your image, it's time to print it out. Select **Print** from the File menu to open the Print dialog box, shown in Figure 13.6.

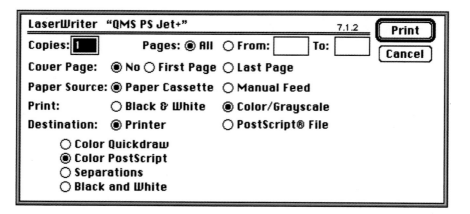

FIGURE 13.6 THE PRINT DIALOG BOX.

The options in this dialog box follow standard printing conventions and are relatively self-explanatory.

The four bottom options allow you to select from the four printing methods supported by Painter:

❏ *Color GDI.* Use this option for printers that use GDI (color or black-and-white), such as many ink-jet printers. Dot gain and halftone screen options do not apply to GDI printers.

❏ *Color PostScript.* Check this option if you use a PostScript printer (most color laser printers, thermal wax printers, imagesetters, and dye-sublimation printers). Dot gain and halftone screen settings apply.

❏ *Separations.* Use this option if you want to print color separations (usually done on an imagesetter) directly from Painter. If you are using your own device, please check your documentation for specific page setup settings. If you are using a service bureau, please contact it for specific instructions before outputting files. This will save them a lot of aggravation due to incorrect settings and will eliminate unnecessary delays.

❏ *Black and White.* This option applies to users of black-and-white laser printers.

When you have made your selections, click **OK** to begin printing.

OUTPUT OPTIONS

A large assortment of printer types is available today; some are affordable, and others are generally more cost-effective if used through a service bureau. You'll have to carefully weigh your needs against cost considerations: black-and-white PostScript laser printers and ink-jet color printers start at less than $1,000 and go up to several thousand dollars; color laser copier systems begin around $60,000; used imagesetters begin at around $10,000, while new ones cost $70,000; thermal wax printers range from a couple of thousand dollars to more than $10,000; dye-sublimation printers begin where thermal wax printers leave off; and Vutek systems (used to print directly onto gessoed canvas) begin at $500,000 (no, that's not a typo).

We'll briefly cover some of the options available, but because technology changes faster than the phases of the moon, we will not be able to cover it all.

We recommend reading the following section, contacting some printer companies for more information (always ask for print samples), and, most important, talking to other people in your field to get first-hand feedback on the advantages and disadvantages of the particular device that interests you.

LASER PRINTERS

Laser printers operate in a fashion similar to photocopy machines. A laser passes over a negatively charged drum, which then attracts negatively charged toner and is rolled over positively charged paper. The paper then passes through a heated roller to adhere the toner to the paper. (Hint: This means that if you get toner on your clothing or carpeting, you can wash it off with cold water. If you use hot water, the toner adheres to the textile as fierce-ly as if it were a piece of paper.)

Laser printers are available for black-and-white as well as color printing. Laser printers are not continuous-tone printers. To print grays or colors, they use a screen, and depending on the resolution of the screen, you'll probably notice the dots.

COLOR LASER COPIERS AS PRINTERS

A number of companies are now using color copiers, via a special raster image processor (RIP), to provide color output. The most prominent copier in this field is the Canon CLC using a Fiery RIP. This technology provides continu-ous-tone images (like a photograph, not using visible dots) and allows a little latitude in your selection of paper. However, thicker paper and highly textured paper may produce questionable results. Depending on the copier, your paper size will range from standard letter-size to legal- or tabloid-size paper.

A color laser copier produces very vivid, sometimes fluorescent, colors. If you are using one as a proofing device for an image that will be reproduced using process printing, keep in mind that process printing does not produce the same vivid results. The closest you can get to accurately reproducing some of these colors will be to print additional PMS colors over the process prints.

If you are simply using the color copier to produce limited edition prints and are not interested in accurate color proofs, this is an excellent choice, although somewhat cost-prohibitive. Color laser prints are available from some service bureaus but are not as common as other types of color prints that provide better color proofing for process color printing. We recommend Iris prints for final pieces and Match prints for color proofing.

THERMAL WAX TRANSFER PRINTERS

Thermal wax transfer printers work more like dot matrix printers than like laser printers. But instead of pins pressing against a ribbon, they press melted wax onto a page, and are much quieter.

Most thermal wax transfer printers provide 300-dpi, noncontinuous prints, with good color coverage. Although not entirely color accurate, they are generally pretty good proofing devices, especially considering that they are affordable enough for many of us to own. This is a good option for artists who do not have large corporate coffers to dig into, do not have large trust funds to tap, or have not (yet) won the lottery.

DYE-SUBLIMATION PRINTERS

Dye-sublimation printers work in a similar fashion to the thermal wax transfer method, except that they provide continuous-tone color coverage. Rather than heat wax and transfer it directly onto the paper, dye-sublimation heats ink, which then turns into gas. The gas is sprayed onto the paper, where it returns to its solid form.

Results from a dye-sublimation printer provide photographic-quality results (sometimes even better than photographs), particularly on smooth, glossy paper. A number of printers work well with a variety of media, including watercolor paper.

Probably the most famous of this type is the Iris printer. Most major service bureaus provide Iris prints. Most dye-sublimation prints, particularly Iris prints, are excellent proofing tools. Many dye-sublimation prints smudge and eventually fade when exposed to sunlight.

There is a catch. Beginning at $10,000 with a per-page print cost of as much as $5, dye-sublimation technology is prohibitively expensive for most artists and small companies to own.

INK-JET PRINTERS

Ink-jet printers use little nozzles to squirt ink onto your paper. The more expensive the ink-jet printer, the more sophisticated a method it uses to squirt the ink.

You get continuous-tone images, but usually with a lower resolution than dye-sublimation printers (as low as 180 dpi), and you have to wait for the ink to dry. Some models may experience clogging of their nozzles and may require special paper. They are generally very quiet machines.

There is good news. Color ink-jet printers can be had for less than $500—or can run up to $5,000. The lower-end ink-jet printers are slower, provide less-accurate color proofing, and have a lower resolution, but you don't have to mortgage the farm to own one.

Many higher-end ink-jet printers now print on substrates such as canvas watercolor paper, handmade paper, embossed sheet metal, and other wild products of your imagination. However, it's a good idea to check with the hardware manufacturer before putting any product of your imagination through your machine, or you may void your warranty.

IMAGESETTERS

Imagesetters provide high-resolution (1,200- to 3,600-dpi) resin-coated (RC) paper or film to make plates for commercial process printing. They are frequently known by their brand names, including Linotronic, Varityper, or Agfa. At a price of $50,000–70,000 new, most of us will never own one, nor will we want to.

SECTION 2

CHAPTER 14

SUSAN LEVAN

ARTIST PROFILE

Susan has an MFA in printmaking and began her career doing editorial illustrations using traditional methods. Her husband and business partner, Ernest Barbee, is an architect and exhibit designer who has been working with Macs since 1984. In 1992, they began looking for a way to work together. The computer seemed a logical connection, so they formed LeVan/Barbee Studio.

Susan uses a Macintosh Quadra 700 with 20 MB of RAM, a 20" SuperMac display with a SuperMac Thunder Light graphics card, a 6" by 9" 609J Hitachi Multipad, and a Tektronix Phaser II SDX (in-house) or IRIS prints (service bureau) to output her artwork.

ON USING PAINTER

In the fall of 1992, we went to pick up some new computer equipment. The salesman was talking about tablets and how much he didn't like them. The minute he described it, I said "I have to try this thing." I sat down at a computer, and the program that was open happened to be Painter. I did a few quick cartoons, and I turned to Ernie and said, "I have to have this." We bought the program and tablet on the spot.

Two things were going on: All of my work, both fine art and illustrative art, is in mixed media. It became obvious that with this particular program, and other digital methods, you can mix all kinds of media that you can't mix in the real world. You can put down a swath of watercolor and cut through it with a scratchboard tool, erase it with an eraser, then paint over it with oil paint. It also seemed to be the answer to our finding a way to work together. Before the tablet and Painter, manipulating the mouse just didn't work for me.

There are so many possibilities with this program, technically, that it is good to start out doing what you know. Do not get caught up in the technical tricks. Explore it like any painting tool. Then, as you feel comfortable, start adding the extra textures and little gizmos you want. It is like any other tool, and needs to be driven by the artists' concepts of work they want to do, rather than by the technology.

STEP-BY-STEP

Security was created as a portfolio piece, and it was used in a Workbook page for Susan's artist rep, Bruck & Moss. It is part of a series of conceptual images.

1. Susan uses a custom color palette set up to create reliable CMYK output. She works directly in Painter from the inception and rarely uses scanned material. She started by drawing the face in black using the Default crayon .

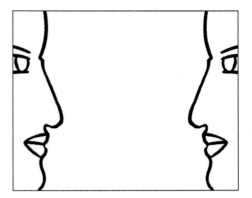

2. Next, Susan created a pattern consisting of signs and symbols, and filled the face using the Paint Bucket tool set to **Clone Source** from the Fill With pop-up menu. She selected **Auto Mask...** from the Mask menu, and chose **Current Color** (black) in the dialog box. She then changed the mask into a selection so she could float the face, flip it horizontally, and fill it with orange.

3. For the face on the right, Susan created a mask using white as the current color and then generated a selection using the Load Selection button on the Mask list palette. She then colored pink and orange inside the selection with the Large Chalk variant using several paper textures. Next, Susan duplicated the original black line floater and filled it with green by selecting the Gel composite

method in the **Controls: Adjuster** palette. When this was done, she dropped the floater.

217

For the face on the left, Susan duplicated the original black line floater, again selected the **Gel** composite method but this time reduced the opacity to 10%. She dropped the floater when she was finished.

4. On the left face, Susan created a mask based on white as she had done before and colored it in blue-green with Large Chalk and a rough paper texture. She then masked the blue-green area and colored it with tan chalk. Her next step was to redraw the eyes and lips using the Default crayon set to black.

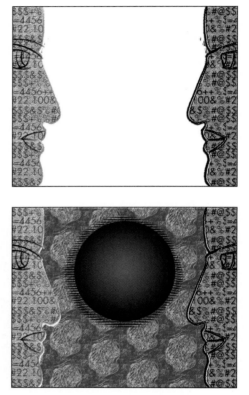

5. Susan chose a blue custom pattern she had previously made to fill the open space between the faces. With the Oval Selection tool she created a dark blue circle in the center of the image and floated it. To give it dimension, Susan opened the **Effects**: **Surface Control**: **Apply Surface Texture...** dialog box and adjusted the light settings. She then drew behind the floating circle in a yellow-orange, again using the Large Chalk, this time selecting **Line 0** for the paper texture.

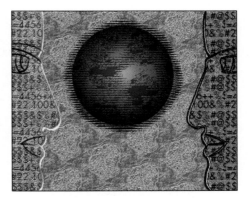

6. To quickly create mask of the background pattern, Susan used the Magic Wand tool set to User Mask. She changed this mask into a selection as she did before, floated it, changed the composite method to **Colorize** on the **Controls: Adjuster** palette, and filled the area with a yellow-gold.

7. In a new file, Susan drew a house in black with the Default crayon and used both the Straight Line and Freehand functions on the Controls palette. She then masked the black area with the same procedure as before, and colored it with red chalk and a rough paper texture.

Next, Susan masked the white area using Auto Mask… set to **Current Color** and then chose **Invert** from the Mask list palette. Susan finds that an inverted mask leaves bits of residue that adds interest. Susan then selected and floated this masked area and used Apply Surface Texture… with the current mask selected in the Using pop-up menu and the Softness slider set to **5.1** so that the lines

She decided to create a drop shadow and accepted the default setting. She then ungrouped the house and shadow floaters, centered the shadow under the floating image, grouped them again, and collapsed them. On the Mask menu she chose **Feather Mask…** and entered **.08** pixels in the dialog box.

Finally, she copied and pasted this newly created image into the main image.

8. In this step, Susan used the Scratchboard tool in black to bring out the facial features.

9. Susan masked the black lines of the faces to create a selection, and then colored them with purple chalk. Next, she select most of background pattern with Magic Wand tool, floated this area and colored into the floater using the Large Chalk variant in both blue-green and blue and yellow. This floater was then dropped.

10. To write the word *security*, Susan chose the **Simple Water** variant of the Water Color brush and modified it in the **Brush Controls: Size** palette by increasing its size to **6.5**. In the **Brush Controls: Water** palette she increased the Wet Fringe slider to **95%**. When this was done, Susan selected **Dry** under the Canvas menu to set the watercolor into the canvas layer.

11. Susan wanted to add a finishing touch to the edges, so with the Large Chalk variant and the Mountain paper texture, she went around the edges of the piece with an orange color. She further eroded the edges by changing the color to white and selecting the **Line 0** and **Line 90** paper textures.

PORTFOLIO

BEATLES

MAN AND DOG

The Flower Dress

Three Businessmen

CHAPTER 15

MARGARET
SWEENEY

ARTIST PROFILE

Margaret graduated from the University of Cincinnati with a degree in graphic design, and went on to work in advertising. Throughout the twenty-odd years of her career, Margaret always painted in her spare time. Four years ago she decided to make the break and devote herself to painting full time.

Several times throughout the year, Margaret travels to different locations, sketching scenery for paintings she'll later do on the computer. "I'm mostly a painter of small towns, simple pleasures, and back roads, because that's what means the most to me."

Margaret then exhibits her work in the galleries and shops near the locales she has visited. She sells her work as limited edition prints. She prefers to make the prints herself to keep control over the process, perfectly duplicating what she sees on the screen by selectively shifting colors where necessary.

In 1995, Margaret was a finalist in Fractal Design Painter's Digital Art Contest, and in 1996 she was the contest's second place winner.

To create her paintings, Margaret uses a Power Mac 7100 AV with 72 MB of RAM, a 5 GB hard drive, a 6" × 8" Wacom tablet, an Apple 14" color monitor, an Apple One scanner, a Tektronix 140 color printer, a LaserWriter Plus, and an Apple color printer. When she makes her prints, she uses the Canon 850 Color Copier with a Fiery interface, and then transfers that print to 140 lb. or 300 lb. cold-pressed watercolor paper.

ON USING PAINTER

Having painted for so many years with the real stuff, I would not have considered painting on a computer if the program did not match the feel of the real brushes and paper. I tend not to use a lot of filters or effects but rather enjoy the brushwork and textures I get from Painter. The pleasure for me comes from creating layer upon layer of strokes with color and texture. I spent a lot of time just experimenting with all the different brush settings in each of the Brushes: Control palettes and now I'm so familiar with them, I don't have to think about it. Even now (I started with Painter 1), I still take the time to go through the Brushes and Paper settings. The Controls palette is an important feature for me because I can build up layers of color and increase the texture with the Opacity and Grain sliders.

Most people are very surprised that my painting are done on a computer, and I'm always asked what I would recommend to others just starting out. First, I tell them it's best to really know the program backwards and forwards because it will free you to focus on what you want to create instead of trying to figure out how to do it. As for reference material, I take close-up photos of details I want to remember, but I don't recommend basing a painting on a scanned photo, unless you deliberately want it to have a photographic feel. The other point I recommend is to keep drawing and painting the real thing because practice will only make you better.

IN THE ORCHARD

Margaret produced this piece for this book, using the steps to emphasize how she generally progresses through a painting. "One of the most frequent questions I get on-line from people who have just started in Painter is how I start a painting. They seem to be more interested in how it evolves than in details, so that's what I've tried to show here."

STEP-BY-STEP

1. Margaret begins by filling an area with a neutral color, then sketches in areas of dark and light to develop shapes and movement, as well as indicate the direction of the light source. She's unconcerned with color or detail at this point, and here used the Gritty Charcoal variant with the Grainy Hard Cover subcategory for drawing. For the paper texture, she scanned in some leaves and then captured them as a paper texture.

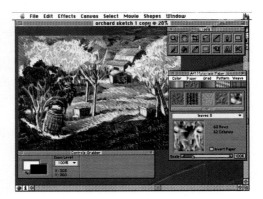

2. Margaret's next phase is to build a base of texture and color for applying brush strokes. Using another leaf scan that had been made into a pattern, and she selected **Surface Control: Apply Surface Texture...** from the Effects menu. From the Using pop-up menu, she chose **Image Luminance** , and set Shine to **1** and Softness to **.5**.

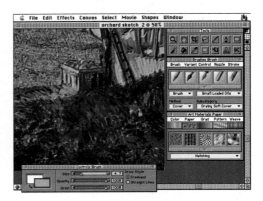

She also added a golden color for the Light Color. She proceeded to paint with Small Loaded Oils with Grainy Soft Cover subcategory, using a low opacity and an increased texture (**Grain** slider to the left), because this allows underlying areas and brush strokes to show through.

3. Working on building up layers of color, pattern, and texture until the painting begins to take form for her, Margaret might use 20 or more combination of brushes while continuing to change paper textures. She might start out with the Rough Out, switch to Gritty Charcoal, and move on to Splatter Airbrush.

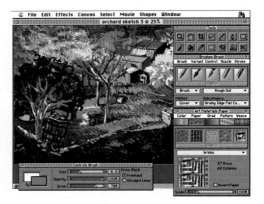

4. For the last stage of cleaning up and adding detail, Maragaret becomes more selective in her brush and paper texture choices, limiting them to only one or two each. In this painting, she used the **Oil** brush with both the **Grainy Soft Cover** and **Grainy Edge Flat Cover** subcategories. She made the **Brick** paper texture by cap-

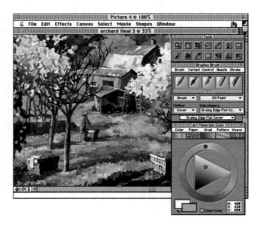

turing a scan of old bricks, which resulted in a texture with a lot of tooth, causing the brush to "catch" on the peaks. To smooth out rough areas, she used the **Brushy** brush.

PORTFOLIO

ORCHARD

BURNIN
LEAVES

Re-creating the feeling of fall experienced on an October trip north, *Burning Leaves* began as a sketch on screen. The color palette was limited to sepia, yellow ochre, and orange for most of the painting, with other colors introduced at the end. The smoke was painted with the Airbrush at various opacities, the wet road with the Water brushes, and the rest with many adjusted variants of oil brushes.

OYSTERS

This painting was done from a sketch on Cedar Key, Florida, of a closed oyster processing plant. The challenge of successfully creating a water color painting on the computer piqued the artist's curiosity enough to re-create the same scene with real water colors, and came up with very similar results.

CHAPTER 16

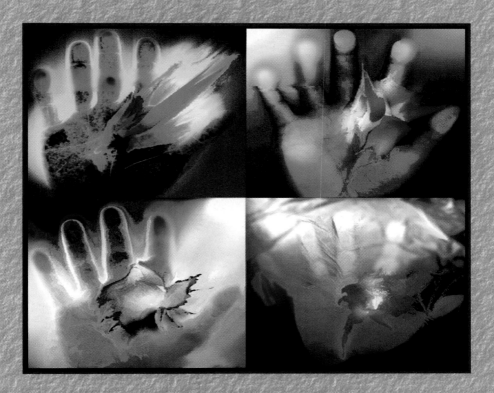

KEN KRUG

ARTIST PROFILE

Ken Krug graduated from the High School of Music and Art in New York City and has a BFA from the San Francisco Art Institute. His professional mainstay is surface (textile) design, but he is equally dedicated to progressing as an artist. This is apparent in his eclectic style. Ken mixes a wide variety of traditional materials and ideas within his computer art. His award-winning textile designs have been featured in several national publications and major motion pictures and television programs, including *Roseanne*, *Big*, *Who's the Boss*, and *When a Man Loves a Woman*. Ken has also had numerous gallery showings of his fine art.

Ken's entrance to the digital art arena is very recent: he bought his system late in 1996. After a moment of panic, Ken took to the computer with a passion, and now says he can't believe how much using it has changed his personal work and his textile design studio work. Over the last few seasons, Ken has started doing a lot of designs with textures and layers, and while he knew he would be able to explore more possibilities in less time, he was really excited by some of the new design directions the computer showed him.

To create his artwork and his surface designs, Ken uses a Power Computing Power Tower Pro 180 with 96 MB of RAM, a 20" Sony monitor, a Umax scanner, and a Wacom drawing tablet. For output, he has an Epson Stylus Pro, and he uses service bureaus for a variety of color prints.

ON USING PAINTER

When I first bought my computer, my experience with computers was very limited, so I had a friend help me set it all up. I tried to get started, but I couldn't get anything to work and felt so overwhelmed that I called my friend and said, "You've got to come back next week and help me take it all down so I can send it back while I can still get my money back."

Fortunately, she said, "Relax, you have a whole month; give yourself some time." Well, I tried to forget about it and not make a decision that day. The next day, I thought, I'm going to send the computer back, but I might as well try to use it one last time. So I opened Painter and started drawing. It felt so natural that I worked straight through until almost 3 AM. I was hooked.

What I like about Painter is that it is a deep program with seemingly endless possibilities, but it's possible to create real works of art using a few basic tools. I found that I could begin by using it intuitively, and only after I became familiar with the program did I go back and read the manual to exploit the program to the fullest.

In fact, my first commercial use of Painter came about two weeks after I bought my computer. I had a job doing a scratchboard of a fish design for a dinnerware

client. I did the dinner plate traditionally with scratchboard, and for the salad plate, I used scans of my scratchboard. By the time I got to the cup, I was creating the design entirely on the computer, using Painter's scratchboard tool. I am still using that same technique.

Another thing I like about Painter is that I can create art that has a funky, non-computer look to it. Currently, I am working with techniques to add a randomness and distressed look to my designs, and Painter is a natural for that. To sum up, computers and Painter now seem as important to my design work as pencils and paint.

STEP-BY-STEP

As a textile designer, Ken thought it would be helpful to show the process of using Painter to create commercial art:

1. The assignment was to create a design for boy's pajamas. Ken began with quick pencil sketches of a motorcycle, a sailboat, a yacht, a plane, and three pairs of sunglasses, knowing that the elements will probably change as the design evolves. He then scanned the motifs at 100 dpi knowing that cloth usually doesn't require a higher resolution for reproduction.

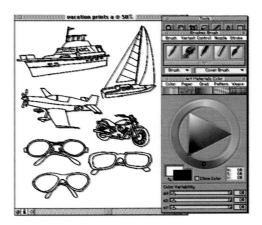

2. Color was the next important consideration. Ken created a new color set consisting of six colors, the maximum number printable for this job, plus white to represent the color of the cloth. The color set was chosen from the Pantone library to reflect CMYK , or printable, values. Next, he opened a new color set consisting of just the dark blue and white, and posterized each scan using this new color set to eliminate all the middle

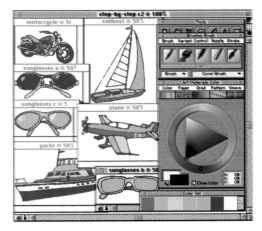

231

tones and give each motif a blue outline. From here he could begin to fill and paint the elements. To add the colors, he used both the Cover brush variant and Paint Bucket tool. To create a softer, more painterly look as he worked, Ken alternated between using **Soften...** from the **Effects: Focus** menu, and **Posterize...,** using the six color set, from the **Effects: Tonal Control** menu. Painter's allowance for many levels of Undo is invaluable at this stage in the design process, when the artist is still experimenting.

3. Ken next made a selection of each motif and arranged them randomly in a new image. The layout shown here is not truly a repeat, but it has that appearance. Ken saved several copies of the layout so that he could play with variations on the basic design.

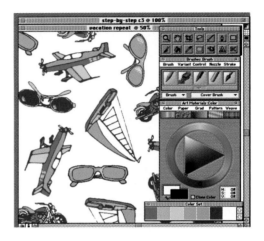

4. First, Ken wanted to distress the design to create texture and to add variation to the white ground. With the ground slected, Ken chose **Apply Surface Texture...** from the **Effects: Surface Control** menu, and created a random pattern of vertical lines by moving the light source to the left side, setting Softness to **20.5**, Amount to **110%**, Picture to **100%**, Shine to **40%**, and Reflection to **5%**. He then went back and applied **Posterize...** with the color set, which colorized the lines, to achieve the result he was after.

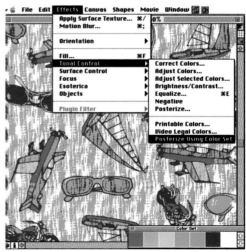

5. For the second look, Ken decided to try the design with a plaid as the ground. Ken opened a file he had of saved plaids and stripes. Each file is one segment of a repeat and is between 2″ and 3″ square. After choosing the plaid for the ground Ken created a new color set consisting of only the pale green and blue from his original color set, plus white. Next, using **Posterize...** with this new

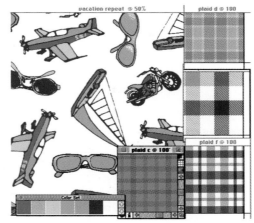

color set, he re-colored the plaid. After selecting a plaid, Ken chose **Capture Pattern...** from the **Art Materials: Pattern** menu to turn the plaid into a pattern.

6. Finally, using the Paint Bucket set to **Clone Source**, Ken filled the ground with the plaid.

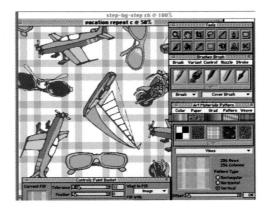

PORTFOLIO

FISH (SALAD PLATE)

SOULS DEPARTING

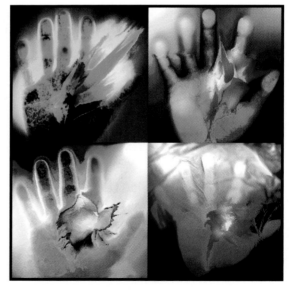

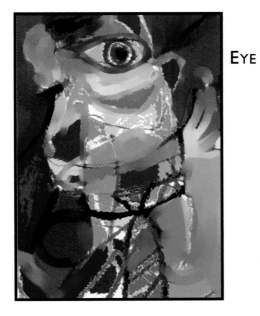

EYE

TAROT CARDS

The Tears

The Energy Ball

CHAPTER 17

DOROTHY SIMPSON
KRAUSE

ARTIST PROFILE

Dorothy is a professor of computer graphics at the Massachusetts College of Art in Boston and Corporate Curator for IRIS Graphics, Inc. She has a bachelor of arts degree in painting (Montevallo University), a master of arts degree in art education (University of Alabama), a doctor of education degree in art education (Pennsylvania State University), and a certificate in management of lifelong education (Harvard University).

Dorothy's recent exhibits have included solo shows at the New England School of Photography, IRIS Graphics, Inc., and the Center for Creative Imaging. Her work has been included in the Seventh National Computer Invitational, Digital Masters at the Ansel Adams Center for Photography, Pixel Pushers Exhibition of Digital Art, SIGGRAPH 94, and Fractal Design Expo 96. Her work was on the January 1995 cover of *IEEE Computer Graphics and Applications* magazine and the February 1995 cover of *Computer Artist* magazine.

Dorothy's work is based on the premise that our similarities are greater than our differences and, at this time in history, electronic media enable us to transcend our separateness and to understand our interdependence. She uses historical and contemporary images, maps showing voyages of exploration, the shifting boundaries of acquisition, and patterns of migration. She embeds in her images the fragments of written language, signs, symbols, charts, and diagrams that are also embedded in our consciousness. She enlarges their fragmented political, ethical, and social meanings by combining, layering, manipulating, and merging them into provocative statements or questions.

Dorothy creates her art using a Quadra 700, with 32 MB of RAM, a 1-GB hard drive, a WACOM tablet, a UMAX UC630 color scanner, a CD-ROM drive, and a SyQuest 44/88/200 cartridge drive. She works concurrently on two monitors, a 14-inch NEC MultiSync and a SuperMac 21-inch, keeping her images on the SuperMac and her menus and notes on the NEC. She proofs to either a HP550C color printer or a Sharp JX730 color printer and produces final output at IRIS corporate headquarters or at a fine arts IRIS printer.

ON USING PAINTER

It's just fabulous because I like working back into my pieces using pastels and other tools. I'll print something out, work with real media to try out some effects, then replicate those effects in Painter.

The Just Add Water brush is wonderful. It allows you to really do some wonderful transitions, smoothing of areas, to actually flow one thing into another. It's also

wonderful to be able to apply textures selectively or to be able to clone using the original luminance of an image.

My work is becoming much more painterly and less photographic in quality, even though I'm still using photographic source images. I think it's actually going to change very dramatically in the next year because I was originally a painter and I really love that quality of Painter.

RENAISSANCE WOMAN

Dorothy incorporates a lot of metallics into her pieces by using Kai's Power Tools, which she says allow for some incredible metallic effects when outputting to IRIS prints. She may also work manually into a print to add additional metallic effects using metallic paint and gold leaf. This image was created for the cover of the January 1997 issue of *International Designers Network* (IdN), published in Hong Kong.

STEP-BY-STEP

1. Dorothy began her piece by opening a painting of a Renaissance woman from Planet Art's Raphael CD, which she flipped horizontally to make space for the IdN logo in the upper-left corner. She cloned the image and filled the clone with Kai's Power Tools Gradient Designer Metallic Gentle Gold. She then used Painter's Apply Surface Texture using Original Luminance to get an embossed effect. A full-scale version became the background image.

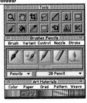

2. Dorothy then made smaller versions of both the Raphael painting and the gold-embossed image. She used the painting as the Clone Source to bring the flesh colors lightly into the embossed image using the Soft Cloner at 50% opacity.

3. For the second small image, Dorothy began with the Raphael painting, copying and pasting it on top of itself using the Composite method at 73% opacity. She then opened a black-and-white drawing from the Zedcor DeskGallery MegaBundle (which is the source of all the drawings in this series). She used **Effects: Tonal Control: Negative** to make the cones white and copied and pasted

them into the second image using Lighten mode at 33% opacity. She applied lighting on the face and upper cones using **Effects: Surface Control: Apply Lighting: Flashy Colors**.

4. The third image used **Edit: Mask: AutoMask** based on the Image Luminance to isolate the lightest part of the figure. The image of the woman was inverted using **Effects: Tonal Control: Negative**, and a drawing of stars was pasted using the Difference Composite method with the woman Masked Outside and the stars Masked Inside so that the stars appear only on the body. A second copy of the woman was pasted over the image using **Composite method: Overlay** at 100%.

5. The fourth image copied the woman and pasted it using the Composite method with the image shifted 2 pixels up and 2 pixels to the left to create a glowing edge. **Effects: Tonal Control: Negative** was used on a drawing of an eye, which was pasted using the default at 100%.

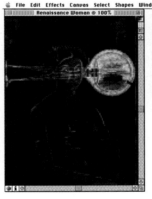

6. The fifth image pasted a second copy of the woman over the original. Using the **Brightness: Contrast** sliders, the Contrast slider was moved all the way to the left, and the Brightness slider was moved all the way to the right. The Composite method Difference, and Opacity was set to 50%. With the woman Masked Inside, an astrologi-

241

cal chart was pasted as the third layer of the image using **Composite method: Darken** at 75%.

7. For the final image, the fifth image was used as the base, and a variety of texture and color options were applied. Dorothy pasted two **Effects: Tonal Control: Negative** drawings of lenses using **Composite method: Difference**. She applied a plain lighting effect at the default setting to give a warmer skin tone and darken the surrounding edge for contrast.

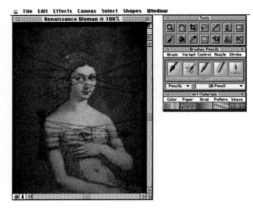

8. The six small versions were assembled across the bottom of the large image. Alien Skin filters were used to apply a drop shadow to the right and bottom of each image.

PORTFOLIO

AGAINST THE WALL

KNEELING AT THE GATE

LADY OF THE FLOWERS

MARKETPLACE

CHAPTER 18

KERRY
GAVIN

ARTIST PROFILE

Kerry graduated from Pratt Institute in 1972 with a BFA in printmaking and a minor in education. He served four years in the Air Force as a graphic designer and then worked in New York as a graphic designer for several publications and ad agencies before moving out on his own 16 years ago.

He is a publications designer and editorial illustrator. His clients include *The Hartford Courant, The New York Times, The Boston Globe, The Chicago Tribune, Industry Week, Publishers Weekly, Byte magazine, Glamour, Ladies Home Journal, MacUser,* and other many publications.

Kerry uses a Macintosh Centris 650 with 64 MB of RAM, a RasterOps 20T Multiscan monitor with a Paint Board Turbo video card, a 12″ × 12″ CalComp graphics tablet, a LaserWriter Select 360 printer for black-and-white proofs, and IRIS color prints from a service bureau to create his digital paintings.

ON USING PAINTER

I've been using the computer in design for the last three years, mostly using QuarkXPress. For whatever reason, I just didn't want to make the jump to computer illustration. Up to then, I used primarily watercolor and pen-and-ink. In the last four years I shifted from traditional watercolor to adding airbrushing. Very recently—the last eight months—I began illustrating on the computer. The very first program I really tried working with was Painter. I read about it in a couple of publications, and it sounded like it was maybe a little more intuitive than some of the more techie-oriented programs, so I sent away for a sample disk.

I played around with it a little bit and really liked it because it was more intuitive. I really responded to that. I worked with it for a few months, and in that time I developed a dozen or so images.

*I find that Adobe Illustrator is object-oriented—it uses shapes and forms—while Painter is very drawing oriented. So I sit down and draw and paint, which is something I haven't done in 20 years. It's a really different process. I feel that Adobe Illustrator draws on my design back*ground, while Painter draws on my painting and drawing background.

STEP-BY-STEP

1. Kerry used a Dover clip-art book on animals (he says they have a book on everything) for reference to sketch the two cows. Because his illustration would be stylized, he only needed a rough sketch. He made floating selections out of each cow so he could later reposition and size them as needed to accomodate the composition. He 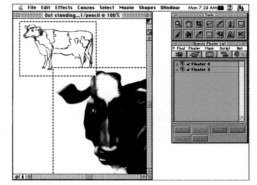 used the Large Chalk tool with the Soft Cover method on Basic Paper for a soft rendered effect.

2. After creating the two cows, Kerry filled in the background with a base color on which to build the meadow. Using the Growth brush and mixing grasses and daisies, Kerry created the field. He also played with the Color palette to keep brighter colors in the foreground, and with the Size palette to reduce the daisies as they receded into 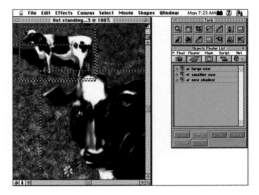 the background. He went in by hand and modified the effect until he was satisfied with (details such as the darkening of the centers of the flowers to make them more realistic). He created a floating drop shadow for the smaller cow, adding a feather to it and reducing its opacity to allow some background to show through.

3. To create the vignette, Kerry dropped all of the floaters, drew a freehand selection around the illustration, and feathered it to 9. Then he cut it out to eliminate the surrounding background.

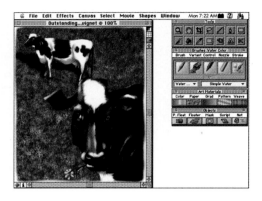

PORTFOLIO

DINNER AT KINTARO

JUSTICE

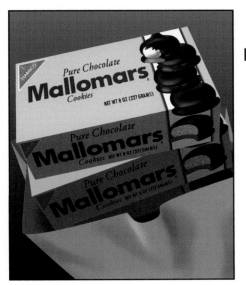

MALLOMARS

ZOE

CHAPTER 19

GARY CLARK

ARTIST PROFILE

Gary is a professional artist and has been a professor at Bloomsburg University in Bloomsburg, Pennsylvania for 24 years, where he teaches computer graphics, drawing, and design. He has a BFA in graphic design, an MA in sculpture, and a Pennsylvania teaching certification. Gary is self-taught on the computer and has been creating computer art for about nine years.

Gary is represented by Silicon Gallery of Philidelphia and Creiger-Dane Gallery of Boston, Massachusetts. His recent exhibitions include a solo exhibition at the Russell Rotunda in the United States Senate Office Building (Washington, DC), a two-person exhibition at Silicon Gallery of Philidelphia, a solo show at 911 Gallery in Indianapolis, Indiana, and a group show at Creiger-Dane Gallery in Boston.

Gary creates his artwork using a Mac Power PC 8100/110 with 81 MB of RAM, an Apple Multiple scan 20" display, a 14" color monitor for palettes, and a Wacom pressure-sensitive pad. The system has a 1-GB hard drive, a Zip drive, and a 44/88 SyQuest drive.

ON USING PAINTER

I first discovered Painter in a magazine review, and then found a colleague at another university who had it on his machine, so I had a chance to play with it. It was just wonderful. It was an analogy to the natural materials I was used to and the interface was pretty straightforward, so it was natural to use. I use natural media now only to enhance what I do with the computer. Sometimes I'll make some studies with inks or dyes or paints, and I may scan those in and use them as part of the work. Or sometimes I'll use them underneath as a template and pull pieces up with the Cloning function.

I show my work, I sell my work. I've been showing nationally and internationally in a mix of traditional and computer art shows. I'm finding that traditional art shows have a lot of trouble finding where to include electronic art. My art might make it into a show as a drawing, as a photograph, or even as a print. I find it depends on the show prospectus how I'll enter the work. I'll even find myself calling to find out what their preferences are in terms of which category the work might fit into. One of my pieces was given a Purchase Award at the Larsen National Drawing Biannual at Austin Peay State University in Clarksville, Tennessee. It was the only computer drawing at the show.

I'm finding you'll have to read the perspective very carefully and have some alternatives for output—I may have the work printed as a photograph and again as an IRIS print. Then, depending on the show, I pick the one that seems more suitable. At one

show in Oregon, I won a prize and there were lots of favorable comments on the work, but the biggest comment was "Can you tell me what an IRIS print is?"

I feel the public has the misconception that the computer makes the work and that you make thousands of prints, but nobody questions someone who makes a silk screen or an etching. So there's this idea that electronic art is infinite and that the computer creates it. I hope one of the things that I've helped to do is to change people's vision of what computer art is. The more people who see electronic art, the more it breaks their misconceptions that computer art is blocky and that the computer creates the art.

WHITE BUFFALO

Gary got the idea for this piece from a newscast about the birth of a white buffalo. Native Americans had been waiting for this event for a long time, and its symbolic content proved irresistible for Gary. He created this piece at a resolution of 150 dpi.

STEP-BY-STEP

1. Gary began by generating land forms in KPT Bryce. He wanted a rocky terrain and spent a lot of time trying different approaches. He finally settled on this one, importing it into Painter to smooth edges and enhance color. The sky was created apart from the land forms from a still digital image photographed using a Kodak/Nikon  DC400 camera. He then worked the sky in Painter using Adjust Colors under Tonal Control as well as the Add Water brush.

2. The swirling effects in the sky were added by cloning a scan of an old exposed glass photographic plate. Gary used a low setting on transparency. The figures were drawn in soft chalk and then splattered with a bristle brush to get the grainy effect. Noise was also added using KPT noise filters.

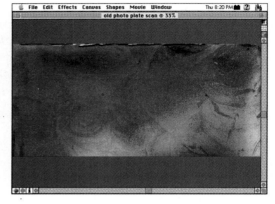

3. Gary had to find a buffalo for reference, so he called an exotic animal farm in his area. He got lucky—they had a buffalo, which he photographed with a digital camera.

4. He cut out this image first by painting a black background. The buffalo was altered to look white by using a combination of tonal controls, including Brightness: Contrast, Posterize, Apply Surface Texture (Paper Grain), and Adjust Surface Controls (Express Texture), which allowed him to play with the image luminance controls.

5. The finished buffalo was cut out and pasted into the main work. The tree was created using a mask he painted into a scan of a paint swatch he made with (traditional) tempera paint. The edges were sprayed white using an airbrush to give it a sense of roundness. He also used the Bleach Eraser and Eraser Darkener to help add contrast throughout the piece. The final work was output as an IRIS print at 24″ × 44″.

PORTFOLIO

Most of Gary's art is created using a combination of Painter, Photoshop, and special effects filters. The landscape forms are generated using fractal mathematics and are pieced and colored in Painter with a variety of tools (Gary's favorites are the Pastels, Distorto, and Water color tools). He used the Cloner feature to modify the basic look of some of his pieces, and Kai's Power Tools for textures and gradients. His skies are shot with a still video camera and then are composited in Painter. Each piece is different, and his method of working and selecting the final output is based on reactions to the ongoing process, his original idea, and how the final output is to be viewed. Gary believes that experience and experimenting are important, and he never finishes a work session without making many new discoveries.

A BUTTERFLY FLAPS
ITS WINGS

APRIL ON THE RIVER

THE PURE SIMPLE
TRUTH

APPENDIX A

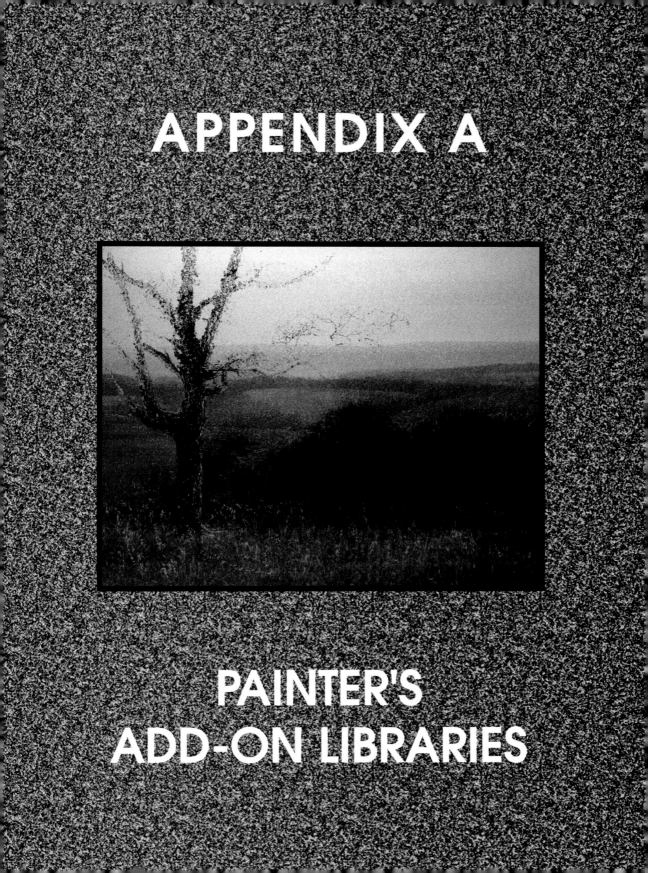

PAINTER'S
ADD-ON LIBRARIES

Fractal Design Corporation, recently renamed MetaCreations, has add-on libraries of textures, brush looks, patterns, floaters, and nozzles to increase your choices when creating art. These CDs are very reasonably priced and are available directly from the company:

MetaCreations
6303 Carpinteria Avenue
Carpinteria, CA 93013
(800) 846-0111 (U.S. and Canada)
(800) 566-6200 (international)

This appendix gives you a sampling of the five libraries.

WILD BUNDLE

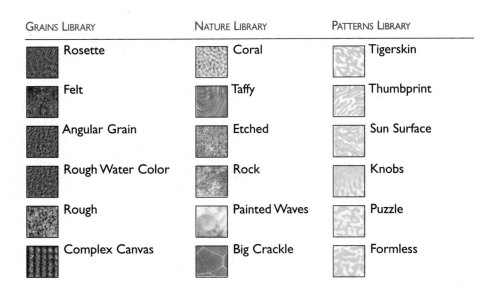

GRAINS LIBRARY	NATURE LIBRARY	PATTERNS LIBRARY
Rosette	Coral	Tigerskin
Felt	Taffy	Thumbprint
Angular Grain	Etched	Sun Surface
Rough Water Color	Rock	Knobs
Rough	Painted Waves	Puzzle
Complex Canvas	Big Crackle	Formless

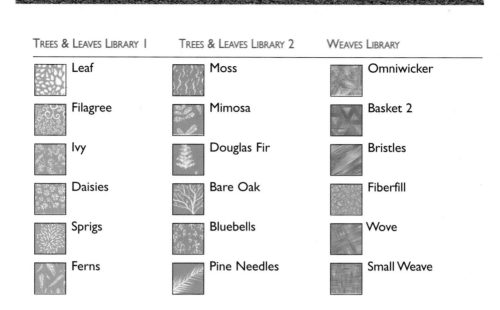

TREES & LEAVES LIBRARY 1	TREES & LEAVES LIBRARY 2	WEAVES LIBRARY
Leaf	Moss	Omniwicker
Filagree	Mimosa	Basket 2
Ivy	Douglas Fir	Bristles
Daisies	Bare Oak	Fiberfill
Sprigs	Bluebells	Wove
Ferns	Pine Needles	Small Weave

BODACIOUS BACKGROUNDS

This CD contains libraries for each of the following:

Wood	Old Paint
Walls	Marble
Slate	Lights
Rust	Leather
Paint	Granite
Old Wood	Fabric

SENSATIONAL SURFACES

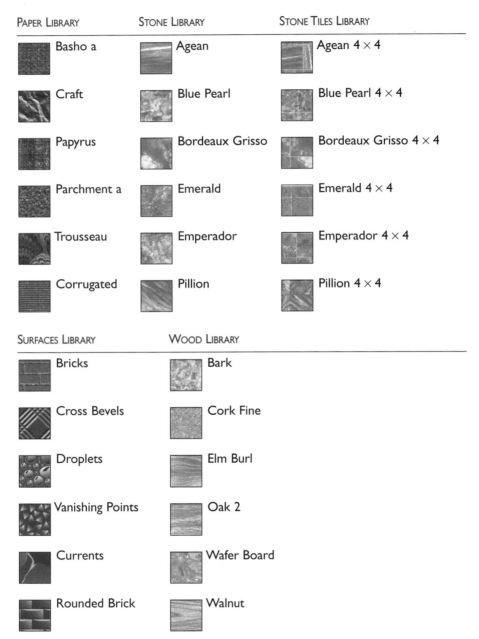

PAPER LIBRARY	STONE LIBRARY	STONE TILES LIBRARY
Basho a	Agean	Agean 4 × 4
Craft	Blue Pearl	Blue Pearl 4 × 4
Papyrus	Bordeaux Grisso	Bordeaux Grisso 4 × 4
Parchment a	Emerald	Emerald 4 × 4
Trousseau	Emperador	Emperador 4 × 4
Corrugated	Pillion	Pillion 4 × 4

SURFACES LIBRARY	WOOD LIBRARY
Bricks	Bark
Cross Bevels	Cork Fine
Droplets	Elm Burl
Vanishing Points	Oak 2
Currents	Wafer Board
Rounded Brick	Walnut

DYNAMIC DUET

MILES OF TILES LIBRARY	RELIEFS LIBRARY	WALLS LIBRARY
Moroccan	African Mask	Metal Mesh
Alhambra	Hieroglyphs	Grating
Japanese	Pillars	Bolt Burst
Roman Cobble	Celtic Snake	Celtic Circles
Glass Brick	Shell Emboss	Deco Scallops
Navaho	Cherubs	Floral

GARDEN HOSE 2

This collection holds textures, patterns, nozzles, and floaters (not represented here).

TEXTURE LIBRARY	PATTERN LIBRARY	NOZZLE LIBRARY
Cattails	Autumn	Clouds
Grape Leaves	Flowers	Reeds
Maggies	Wildberries	Birch
Sweetgum	Birch	Marguerites

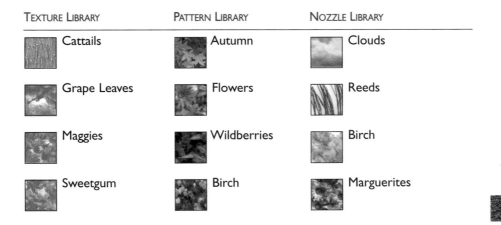

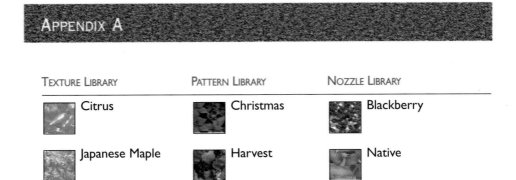

TEXTURE LIBRARY	PATTERN LIBRARY	NOZZLE LIBRARY

Citrus

Christmas

Blackberry

Japanese Maple

Harvest

Native

INDEX

ABOUT THE CD-ROM

The *Fractal Design Painter 5* CD-ROM contains:

A LIBRARY OF STOCK PHOTOS

A wide array of images from Image Club Graphics (a division of Adobe Systems, Inc.) and PhotoDisc, Inc. is on the CD. All of these images have been saved in the TIFF format and can be accessed by Macintosh and Windows 95 users.

PAINTER 5 DEMO

The CD contains a demonstration version of Painter 5 for the Macintosh. Unfortunately, we were not able to include a Windows 95 demo at the time this book was going to press.

Windows 95 users can download a Painter 5 demo from the company's Web site, free of charge, at: **http://www.fractal.com** or **http://www.metacreations.com**.

Please note that the demo versions of Painter do not print or save your files, nor will they record a session. Macintosh users must be running System 7.5 or later to use the demo.

Please refer to the contents of this book for instructions on how to create a new document, open existing documents, and use Painter's vast palette of features.

SAMPLE ANIMATION FRAMES

A folder containing several animation frames that have been created in Painter is also on the CD.